PRAISE FOR IN

"*In The Trenches is addictive – each page and chapter so rich in detail that it is mesmerizing.*" *(Andrew Alexander, former Ombudsman, the Washington Post.)*

"*Adams's life looked very short when as a teenager he led an infantry platoon through a Korean War minefield by moonlight. But what followed was a long, luminous and original career in journalism and public affairs counseling. I can't think of anyone else who saved a Roman temple from London bulldozers, wrote news for Walter Cronkite and the other grandees of network television, advised Polish President Lech Walesa, and flew to Alaska for damage control after the Exxon Valdez disaster. 'In The Trenches' is an exciting story, well told – a great read.*" *(Lee Smith, FORTUNE magazine Board of Editors (retired.)*

"*John Adams has had a ringside seat as a journalist and respected Washington public affairs counselor to major events from the Battle of Britain to the latest battles for cybersecurity. 'In The Trenches' offers fresh behind-the-scenes facts and insights that have shaped today's world.*" *(Gil Klein, Assistant Professor, American University School of Communication; author, 'Reliable Sources: 100 Years at the National Press Club.')*

"*It was with joy that I fell upon this beautifully crafted book – a great journalist's oh-so-readable memoir. It's all here: World War II, Fleet Street, the Korean War, Radio Free Europe, Africa, the Nixon Administration and inside ABC and CBS News. A true tour de force.* (Llewellyn King, syndicated columnist and co-host of White House Chronicle TV.)*

"*John Adams has given us an enormously useful treatise on the world of corporate communications that reads with the intrigue of an historical novel and the crispness of LeCarre prose.*" *(Anthony Weir, co-author of "Get Me The White House.")*

"John Adams is regarded as a statesman in America's public relations profession. Many of us have listened, learned and followed his lead toward effective media engagement and public support." (E. Bruce Harrison, Counselor and Adjunct Professor, Leadership Communications, Georgetown University.)

"When communications legend John Adams speaks about public relations, smart people listen. When he writes a book, smart people read it. In this volume, he shares with us his journey from child evacuee during the London Blitz to one of this country's most influential public affairs professionals." (Ben Zingman, Ph.D., Adjunct Professor of Strategic Public Relations, Graduate School of Political Management, The George Washington University, D.C.)

"In The Trenches is a humorous, charming and warm memoir that, unlike so many Washington books, is both honest and interesting. John Adams talks less about himself than about the events that have shaped him and the world during his lifetime. It is a wonderful tale, well told. A truly special book that you should not only read, but buy for your friends. They will thank you. " (John Fogarty, former Senate press secretary, White House reporter and president of the National Press Club.)

In the Trenches

Adventures in Journalism and Public Affairs

John Adams

iUniverse, Inc.
Bloomington

In the Trenches
Adventures in Journalism and Public Affairs

iUniverse books may be ordered through booksellers or by contacting:

iUniverse
1663 Liberty Drive
Bloomington, IN 47403
www.iuniverse.com
1-800-Authors (1-800-288-4677)

ISBN: 978-1-4620-6783-1 (sc)
ISBN: 978-1-4620-6784-8 (hc)
ISBN: 978-1-4620-6785-5 (e)

Library of Congress Control Number: 2011960596

Printed in the United States of America

iUniverse rev. date: 03/06/2012

To Caroline, Judy, Wilf and Patricia.

Contents

Foreword

John Adams has written a fascinating book about his life, but it's also a book about what's happened to journalism. Today's news ecosystem thrives on morsels of information that spread with astonishing speed. Gone is the era when news was filtered through a select number of gatekeepers. In its place is a new way of knowing. Information now arrives in the palm of the hand, instantaneously and, sadly, often unedited.

It's unwise to disparage this "new journalism." True, newspapers may be dying. And the concept of "appointment television," when we waited for the evening network newscast to learn the day's major events, may be fading. But the future of journalism, with all of its imperfections and uncertainties, is bright and exciting. More people have access to more information than ever before. That's because in the Digital Age, the entry barriers to journalism are virtually nonexistent. At one time, those with ink, paper, and a costly printing press controlled the flow of information. Later, over-the-air broadcasts were restricted to a relative few with a government-issued license. But with the Internet, those who wish to engage in journalism are limited only by their creativity and the extent of their labors.

Alas, journalistic quality and quantity are different matters. Much of what passes today for journalism is little more than what is being talked about. Many news websites are heavy on aggregation, linking to information that may or may not be true. Too often, something is "news" simply because it has been asserted. Information is affirmed, but not verified. Truth is sacrificed. Credibility suffers.

That sad reality leads us back to the extraordinary life that John Adams has chronicled in this book. Today, he is best known as the head of John Adams Associates, the well-established communications and public affairs firm that he founded in the nation's capital. With a team of specialists, he provides counsel to Fortune 500 companies, nonprofit institutions, and industry associations.

But at his core, Adams is a journalist—and a darn good one. He started his career literally as a child in England during World War II as publisher of the *Three Alpha News* in a small town not far from London. As a profit-making enterprise, it was a disaster. Paper was in short supply and commercial printing was prohibitively expensive, so the idea was to produce a single copy and convince people to pay a penny to read it. "This turned out not to be a good business model," Adams writes with droll understatement, but "it was fun to do, and it introduced me to the magic of journalism."

Adams had caught the bug, and he soon went far and high. By age fourteen, he had penned an article that appeared in the *Daily Mirror*, then Britain's largest newspaper with a circulation of four million. In his later teens as an apprentice reporter for a local weekly, he covered a visit of twenty-five-year-old Queen Elizabeth II. After military service in Korea, at the ripe old age of twenty, he went to London's Fleet Street as a scribe for the highly regarded *Daily Telegraph*. Soon he was reporting from Paris, and then on to Munich and Bonn with Radio Free Europe. Still a young man, he traversed the pond to New York and an editorship with the influential *Catholic News*. From his new home, he landed key positions with ABC News and, later, CBS News, during the Golden Age when television was emerging as the nation's most powerful medium.

From these perches, whether newspaper reporter or network news producer, Adams had a ringside seat on world events. Combined with his later government service in the Executive Office of the President, as well as his representation of high-profile clients in the private sector, he has interacted with some of the leading public figures of the last half century. Few have had the opportunity to chat over sherry with the Duke of Wellington or interact with famed broadcast journalist Edward R. Murrow. How many journalists have been privileged to work at the elbow of legendary ABC News anchor Howard K. Smith or to write scripts for CBS News anchor Walter Cronkite, "the most trusted man in America"?

Adams has witnessed an extraordinary swathe of history, from well-documented world events to lesser-known episodes that reveal the character and oddities of leaders on the world stage. He was on hand in Berlin during the Cold War when Vice President Lyndon B. Johnson curiously handed out ballpoint pens bearing his name to Germans who wanted instead to be assured that the United States would stand by them against Soviet expansionism. He crafted news coverage of Konrad Adenauer, the remarkable eighty-year-old chancellor of postwar Germany who cultivated roses as a hobby because it taught him patience, "the most important thing in politics." He viewed conservative Republican delegates relentlessly booing Nelson Rockefeller in San Francisco at the 1964 GOP convention because they considered him too liberal. And he felt the ire and witnessed the controlling impulses of a young Donald Rumsfeld, upset with Adams's approach to a routine public relations initiative when the two worked in the Nixon administration.

All of this is laid out in a book that is personal, anecdotal, and highly readable. It is also addictive, each page and chapter so rich in detail that it is mesmerizing. Together, it recounts the life and times of someone blessed by the opportunity to witness the pages of history literally turning.

In that regard, it is journalism in its purest form. The events that Adams has recounted are not recycled, nor are they unverified. They are not based on a video news feed or a press pool report. Rather, they are descriptions and recollections that are vivid, accurate, unfiltered, authentic. They are, in a sense, the "old journalism," where firsthand accounts were prized hallmarks of reportorial excellence. Adams saw it all with his own eyes, heard it with his own ears. He lived it.

—**Andrew Alexander,** Former Ombudsman
for *The Washington Post* and Washington
Bureau Chief for Cox Newspapers

Bombs, Big Ben, and the Three Alpha News

It was the summer of 1939 – one of the better summers in England – when soldiers suddenly invaded our local park and started digging trenches.

This made games of hide-and-seek much more fun, until the trenches got too deep and we couldn't get out without help. We were warned not to play in them anymore.

What were the trenches for? "The war," they told us. But in August there was no war, just endless sunny days. And even if there was a war, what would the trenches do to stop it? We couldn't figure it out.

Did they expect the Germans just to fall into the trenches and surrender? Or did they expect our families to hide in the trenches? We were finally told that the trenches were to help soldiers defend the balloon station in the center of the park.

The balloon station was fun. Soldiers kept inflating and deflating huge, silver, Dumbo-like balloons, called barrage balloons. They sent the inflated ones hundreds of feet into the air, then brought them down again, then up again, all the time adjusting the wires that tethered them to the ground. My school pals and I were lost in wonder. We did not want to go home. We wanted to help with the balloons.

Ours was just one of many balloon stations all over London that eventually created a giant silver canopy over the city, a magical sight. The idea was to deter German planes from flying over the city, or from flying so low that they would get entangled in the multiple wires of the balloons.

As we excitedly discussed all of this, we were brought up against a new reality. Our school was about to be evacuated to an unknown destination. Here was another new adventure about to begin. As we boarded a special train, we had no idea how long our journey would be. As it turned out, the journey wasn't too long, just an hour or two to a station called Hemel Hempstead and Boxmoor, which we had never heard of. After a headcount to make sure no one had been lost, we boarded buses that took us to a large church hall, where we all sat on the floor waiting for local residents to come by and decide which of us they were willing to accept into their homes. It was a long wait. Girls were preferred since they were expected to be better behaved. I was among the last group of ragtag boys. As the hall emptied, we began to wonder what would happen if no one claimed us. Would they send us back to London? Finally, a billeting officer showed up and said she had found someone willing to take us in.

Two days later, on Sunday morning, September 3, war was declared.

A fellow evacuee and I were fishing for tiddlers in a river near our new home when three piercingly loud sirens sounded just before noon. We were not sure what the sirens were for until a man passing by told us they meant war had started with Germany. He advised us to go home. As seven-year-old Londoners, we had never seen a natural river or stream before and were reluctant to give up our newfound activity, war or no war. We could see no bombers overhead and doubted that they could see us. But eventually everything became eerily quiet, so we knew something must be up.

Where was home? At this point, it was a tiny four-room row house to which four of us boy evacuees had been sent to live with a truck driver's family in this country town of Hemel Hempstead, about twenty-five miles northwest of London. The driver's wife was a warm, loving woman with two children of her own. She took great care of us and was a lot less bossy than our own mothers, whom we had left behind in London, and who still had no idea where we were.

Children below school age, such as my three-year-old brother, were evacuated with their mothers at a different time and to a different place. In our case, they were sent to Bletchley, another country town about seventy miles away, where they were "billeted" with the local vicar and his wife, who were far less welcoming than our truck driver's wife. The vicar treated my mother as free kitchen help and accommodated her in the servants' quarters. She was not allowed to use the phone and allowed out for a walk only with special permission. It was a miserable situation. The lack of phone communication was a problem for many families who had been suddenly evacuated, without knowing their final destination. Phones were by no means as universal as they are today. My father was still living at our flat in London, but had no phone and no car. Eventually, he discovered where we all were and how to reach us by bus and train.

This meant my freedom was coming to an end. Meantime, on weekend mornings, I had acquired a job helping Horace, an elderly milkman, deliver milk to the neighborhood. His milk cart was pulled by an equally elderly horse who knew exactly where to stop and start without any word from anyone. Again, having freshly arrived from London, where few horses were to be seen, I found this whole scene totally fascinating.

Eventually, to our chagrin, our school reorganized itself and we were called to classes. Our new schoolhouse was a large, drafty Victorian building that had been scheduled for demolition. Nothing worked, including the toilets. There was no school furniture, so we were instructed to bring newspapers to sit on during class. This was all still a great adventure, especially when the weather turned cold and our classrooms were warmed by huge coal fires, around which we sat drinking our milk and eating lunch as if on a picnic.

After a few weeks some secondhand desks arrived, and we settled into a more regular routine. Our first school reader was *Les Misérables*, a bit heavy for our age level, but probably the only book available in sufficient quantities. I developed a great admiration for our teachers, who were also evacuees, but performed the role of foster parents and tried to make life as pleasant as possible for us.

At age ten, I was lucky enough to win a scholarship to our local secondary school, the Hemel Hempstead Grammar School, a fairly new school that already had established a strong academic reputation and is still ranked among the best in the country, though to the dismay of many alumni it eventually dropped the word *Grammar* in its name.

By now, my mother, father, and younger brother had discovered our hideaway and rented a house nearby, where we all lived together for the rest of the war. My father, a veteran of World War I, commuted to London six days a week, where he managed a department store, and served as an air raid warden during his time off. When my brother was old enough to go to school, my mother took a job making bomb cases. There was no shortage of jobs. It seemed that every family in England was engaged in the war effort in one way or another.

Hemel Hempstead was close enough to London that we could see the sky lit up with searchlights and fires as the German bombing raids increased. An aunt's coffee-roasting business in central London was bombed. Fortunately, she was not hurt, but for the next several weeks she carried on her roasting business with no roof and only half a wall. The noise from the anti-aircraft guns was often much louder and more frightening than that of the bombs.

Hemel had its own colossal searchlight, operated by a team of young women soldiers with whom we enjoyed flirting on our way home from school while waiting for night to fall. We were not a main target of the enemy bombers, but we were close enough to the American air base at Bovingdon that we attracted occasional attention. We often awoke to sirens warning that German bombers were in the area and we became quite expert at identifying the distinctive throb of their engines. Our house had no basement, so if the bombers seemed to be getting too close, our parents would insist that my brother and I sleep on a mattress beneath the staircase – the safest place, apparently, if the house was hit.

"This is London"

My journalistic career began almost immediately. Because of the war, we were all intensely interested in the news. Each morning, we learned from the radio about the previous night's bombing attacks, which cities had been hit, the number of casualties, how many German planes had been shot down, and how many of our own were missing. In the evening, we never missed the BBC's main newscast of the day, the *Nine O'Clock News*, which led off with the reassuring chimes of Big Ben and was followed by the news in French for the men of the Maquis, the French resistance. This was preceded for several minutes by a stirring drumbeat of the Morse signal for *V* (for Victory) and the announcer's dramatic words, *Ici Londres* (This is London). My spine still tingles when I think about it. For us kids, it was beyond exciting; it made us feel part of a worldwide struggle between good and evil.

There was also a darker side, when classmates' families received official letters notifying them that their fathers or brothers had been killed or wounded in action. One morning, a close friend learned that his father had lost his life when the Germans scored a direct hit on his warship, the HMS *Hood*, killing virtually all on board. Another friend's brother was killed in jungle fighting in Malaya. In my own family, a cousin was seriously wounded and decorated for bravery in France, and a half brother was wounded in the Norwegian campaign. Meanwhile, an occasional bomb exploded too close to the school, sending us all scampering to the basement, where classes continued among walls of sandbags. Tough for the teachers to make themselves heard. Great fun for us kids.

Against this background, it was often difficult to focus on the intricacies of French grammar or English poetry, although there was a line in one poem that we all remembered, from the poet Rupert Brooke, who had died in World War I. "If I should die," he wrote, "think only this of me: that there's some corner of a foreign field that is forever England." He did die in a foreign field, and at that point in our lives, we felt there was every chance that we might soon follow him.

It was against this background, too, that I became an amateur journalist—as founder, publisher, and editor of the *Three Alpha News*, our class newspaper, written and illustrated by hand and circulated for a penny a look. The school had no printing press, paper was in short supply, and we could not afford a commercial printer, so we made one copy and hoped people would pay a penny to read it. This turned out not to be a good business model, but it was fun to do and it introduced me to the magic of journalism.

Then—at age fourteen—I had my first article published in a national newspaper. The war had just ended, and I wrote about the election fever then gripping the country, including me. I wrote it by hand after doing my homework one evening and mailed it in to the four-million-circulation *Daily Mirror*, then Britain's biggest newspaper. I did not expect to hear back, and I didn't. We had no phone at home. But about a week later, a neighbor told me she had read it and congratulated me. When I saw it in the paper, I was embarrassed—the editors had given it a huge headline, and the article filled most of a page. Quite a large check soon followed. It was at this point, I think, that I decided to become a journalist. It did not seem too difficult.

My journalistic education really began when my cousin, Patricia FitzGerald, a gifted writer who should have been a journalist but became a wartime nurse instead, gave me a copy of the autobiography of a distinguished British correspondent named Philip Gibbs, one of the great frontline reporters of World War I. After that, I read every book I could find on the subject in the local public library—and the more I read, the more exciting the prospect became. Journalists seemed to lead wonderful lives, filled with adventure, dealing with important matters and important people, influencing events, and enjoying the warm comradeship of fellow journalists. One of the greatest attractions, for me, was that there were no barriers to entry. No exams. No university degree required. The only academic requirement was that you should know or be willing to learn shorthand (tape recorders were as yet unknown).

So when the time came for me to leave school, just after my sixteenth birthday, I became an apprentice reporter on the local weekly paper, the *Hemel Hempstead Gazette*. This, I understood, was the normal way to start. In those days, few journalists ever attended a university. We liked to boast that our university was the "real world." The *Gazette* was housed in a once-grand Edwardian mansion on the main street. The owner and his family, wonderfully kind and generous people, lived upstairs. The offices were on the ground floor. A large office was assigned to the advertising and business staff and a smaller one to the editorial staff, consisting of a news editor and two reporters, of which I was now one. The only typewriter and only phone were in the advertising office, so we wrote all our copy by hand, and instead of asking permission to use the phone, we usually opted for face-to-face meetings with our sources. Since it was a fairly small town, this was easy enough.

"Names Make News"

My first reporting assignment was to find and interview the delivery man of a local liquor store, who was also secretary of the Old Contemptibles. This was an organization of World War I veterans that proudly derived its name from Kaiser Wilhelm's description of Britain's "contemptible little army"—an army that eventually helped win the war. My story was considered satisfactory, so I was given a more important assignment—writing the weekly "Kiddies Corner" under the pen name of Uncle George. This was a task for Saturday mornings. On Saturday afternoons, I covered local events such as flower shows and soccer matches, which I had to write up on Sundays to provide early copy for the printers on Monday morning. Altogether, there was not much free time. But I loved every minute.

One of the great things about working for a local paper, I discovered, was that you were a key person in the community. Without you, most people wouldn't know what was going on, and their prize chrysanthemums and dahlias would go unremarked, as would the winners of the darts matches in the pubs, the village whist drives, and the local weddings. "Names make news" was our mantra, so we always mentioned as many people as possible. You also learn a great deal about your town and how it works. You discover that the mayor—usually a key news source with an outsize ego—expects to appear in at least one flattering photo each week, preferably on the front page. I later discovered that clergymen, even bishops and cardinals, shared the same desire for worldly recognition and confirmation of their importance. This came as something of a surprise.

The biggest story I ever had to cover for the *Gazette* was the visit of Queen Elizabeth II, then just twenty-five years old. This was one of her first public appearances, and everybody wanted to be seen with her and to talk with her. She had a porcelain-like quality, very gentle and strikingly beautiful, and, like her much-revered mother, found time for everybody. To use the terminology of the day, her smile was "radiant," and she bestowed it generously on everyone. The visit was a great success. She was the first monarch to visit the town since Henry VIII and Anne Boleyn stopped by in 1539, when the king granted the town its royal charter. I was the only reporter covering the Queen's visit for our paper, which presented quite a logistical challenge, since her automobile route was some three miles long and I was on foot. Though I ran pretty fast, I couldn't be everywhere to catch what she did or said. Fortunately, we also had a photographer with a bicycle, so our coverage was primarily photos and captions—and headlines.

Another big story that came my way was the discovery of medieval wall paintings in a cottage just outside the town, in a hamlet called Piccotts End. These five-hundred-year-old religious scenes were found when a young couple moved in and decided to scrape the walls before applying new wallpaper. The priceless frescoes were unfortunately damaged by spear marks, said by experts to have been made by Cromwell's soldiers when marauding through the area attacking religious symbols—adding, nevertheless, to the historical interest. It became a great story for the national press, and the group of historic cottages went on to become a major tourist attraction, which they still are today. I discovered that being the first to find stories and tell the world about them is part of the true joy of journalism.

Merry Christmas

Perhaps the most satisfying of all the stories I wrote in my first year as a reporter concerned a Polish refugee family that was being evicted from a building on the grounds of a local convent—just before Christmas. I knew the convent well; it was where I had taken my catechism classes. As I looked into the circumstances, it appeared that the Mother Superior had decided that the convent needed the building where the family was living for additional storage space, regardless of the fact that the family had nowhere to go. Housing was in very short supply everywhere, and the Poles had very little money. I wrote up the story, including the nuns' explanation that they needed the space for storage. The situation seemed to me to be almost biblical. And the nuns had taught me well enough that I found their lack of humanity in this instance to be quite unconscionable. As it happened, there was a happy ending. A landlord who had read my story offered the family a small house virtually free of charge. On Christmas Eve, the family invited me to join them. They had little furniture, but had a huge Christmas tree in their new living room. They were extremely happy. I was touched by their gratitude and have always remembered this incident as a small example of the power that journalists have to influence events and do good in the world.

One day, soon after the Korean War had started, I attended a lecture sponsored by our local United Nations Association. The speaker was billed as a colonel in the U.S. Army. The event was chaired by the mayor and held in the hall of our largest Baptist church. All very proper. But as the speaker launched into his talk, it became obvious that this was not what the audience had come to hear: it was instead a long diatribe against the United States as the "real aggressor" in Korea, and how Britain should denounce U.S. policy and demand that U.S. troops be withdrawn as soon as possible so that South Korea could again be free. I was astounded. I had followed the developing tensions in the Korean peninsula fairly closely, and none of what the speaker said rang true. At the end of the meeting I talked briefly to the mayor, who said he had been equally shocked. I asked him how the speaker had been chosen, and he explained that he had been strongly recommended by one of their members—a certain Mr. Wolfe, a biology teacher at my old school, who, I knew, also happened to be secretary of the local Communist Party.

The next day I got permission to use the phone in the *Gazette*'s business office and called the U.S. embassy in London. I asked if they had any information on the speaker, the supposed U.S. Army colonel. They did not, and later they called me back to say the U.S. Army had no record of such an individual. In short, he was a phony. I then quizzed the mayor some more on how this whole event had come about. I talked to others who had attended the session and were equally upset. I now had my story. The page-one headline declared that the local UN Association had been the victim of a hoax, misrepresenting the credentials of the speaker and essentially doing the bidding of the local Communist Party. Communists in Britain at that time were much more active than in the United States and were the source of many false stories in the media. The paper did not receive any official protests from the "colonel" or the Communist Party, though I heard from one of his students that the biology teacher, Mr. Wolfe, was very upset, describing the story as "shoddy journalism." What else could he say? I have been wary ever since of the left-leaning United Nations Association and its various offshoots.

Among our local celebrities were Stirling Moss, the world champion race-car driver, and his younger sister, Pat, a champion horsewoman who also became a world-class driver. I did not know about public relations at the time, so was quite surprised by the number of photos we received of them both—clear, sharp action photos that did much to liven our pages. We also had claims to literary fame, beyond the fact that Francis Bacon had once lived in the town. The acerbic Irish playwright George Bernard Shaw lived locally. And the whimsical Catholic philosopher and essayist G. K. Chesterton, author of the *Father Brown* detective stories, lived nearby in the neighboring county of Buckinghamshire. They were two of the greatest writers of their time, Shaw garnering the Nobel Prize for literature as well as an Oscar for adaptation of his play *Pygmalion* into *My Fair Lady*—the only writer ever to receive both awards. Plus, our local prep school had many distinguished students, ranging from Lord Louis Mountbatten, who became the last viceroy of India, to the Nawab of Pataudi, one of the world's all-time greatest cricketers, who for several years captained India's national team.

So though we were only a small local weekly with a circulation of seven thousand, we felt that greatness was all around us. And London was only twenty-five miles away. We were able to augment our slim salaries with occasional reporting projects for the major national dailies. These included a regular weekly assignment to phone in the local soccer results as soon as the games were over. It was probably the easiest money I ever made.

Many journalists are happy to spend their professional lives as historians of their communities, recognized and respected, with regular lives and friendships, escaping the stress and disruptions that often accompany more challenging assignments in the uncharted waters of what we like to call the "major media." I was not one of them. I was restless for broader horizons. The government soon obliged.

The Queen Mum and Korea

In Britain in the 1950s, all young men were required to do two years of national service. You could choose to join the army, navy, or air force. I chose the navy, but soon discovered that it didn't matter what you chose, you were sent where you were most needed—which, for most of us, meant the PBI (poor bloody infantry). It seemed to be just a question of whether you would be fighting communist guerrillas in the jungles of Malaya, the *mau mau* in Kenya, or the Chinese in Korea. So, soon after reaching the age of eighteen, I was "called up" and began a ten-week course of basic training in Colchester, an ancient garrison town near the east coast that was once the capital of Roman Britain. There I learned to shoot, throw hand grenades, conduct bayonet charges, dismantle, clean, and reassemble weapons, march in formation—and salute. The barracks where we slept had evocative names of the old days of empire like Hyderabad and Kandahar. Socially, we were organized into platoons of roughly twenty-five men each and came from all walks of life. Britain was still a very class-conscious society, and I found that getting to know my fellow recruits and the lives they led before joining the army was one of the most interesting aspects of our training.

My life changed somewhat for the better when I was chosen by the War Office Selection Board for three days of tests to see if I was fit for training to be an officer. The tests were stressful, mentally and physically, as we were presented with a series of obstacles and observed every moment to see if we demonstrated sufficient initiative, leadership, and other boy scout–type qualities. Luckily, I passed the course and soon thereafter was sent to infantry-officer training school at Eaton Hall in Cheshire for another sixteen weeks of training. Eaton Hall itself was a stately old Victorian mansion set among acres of beautiful grounds. It was on loan to the government from its owner, the Duke of Westminster, one of Britain's wealthiest men. It was opulent in every way, and it made you feel opulent just by being there. It had an organ fit for a cathedral, which one of the cadets played magnificently. My fellow cadets were mostly from very wealthy and well-known families and had been educated at some of the nation's most famous private schools. For those sixteen weeks, I felt like a guest in a privileged world.

I graduated as a second lieutenant shortly before my nineteenth birthday. Our graduation dinner with the commandant of the training school was a very formal affair, held in the beautiful, high-ceilinged dining room of Eaton Hall. It made us feel quite important. The commandant sat at the head of a very long table, and we were arrayed on either side. After dessert and before he began to address us, waiters brought glasses of port and placed them carefully on the table in front of each of us. Since I didn't drink alcohol, I asked the waiter serving me to remove the glass of port and bring me something nonalcoholic. He brought an orange drink in a rather large glass. I did not realize how much this stood out— fifty-nine small glasses of port interrupted by a tumbler of orange squash— until the waiter returned a few moments later, removed the orange drink, and placed another glass of port in front of me. When I asked him what was going on, he told me quietly, "The commandant said, sir, that you'll drink port and like it."

I decided I was not in a position to win this battle and didn't want to put my graduation on the following day at risk, so I drank the port and liked it. I concluded that this must be part of my training to be an officer in the British army.

The next day, there was a grand passing-out parade with a military band and flags of all kinds, watched by hundreds of proud parents who had driven from all parts of the country in their Bentleys, Daimlers, and Armstrong Siddeleys. When the parade was over, the parents and their uniformed offspring mixed with senior officers and other well-to-do parents at a buffet to the side of the parade ground, sipping the ritual Pimm's, which seemed to have been invented for just this sort of occasion. They then packed their sons' belongings into their cars and drove them home. *This was a wonderful occasion, something we do really well in this country,* I thought to myself with genuine pride as I hitched a ride to the railroad station in the back of an army truck. My parents had not been able to attend the ceremony.

After a few days' leave, I joined my regiment, the Bedfordshire and Hertfordshire Regiment, at the School of Infantry in Warminster, not far from Stonehenge on the perpetually windswept Salisbury Plain. The regiment was responsible for demonstrating various infantry tactics such as "platoon in attack," "platoon in defense," and house-to-house fighting. Our audience consisted of visiting officers from all parts of the world.

It was here, after the day's exercises, that I learned about the social side of being an army officer, from issuing invitations and entertaining guests at cocktail parties to formal regimental dinners, where seating plans were carefully drawn up and the one-hundred-year-old regimental silver was brought out for all to admire. The Queen Mother was our honorary colonel, and at regimental dinners the first toast always honored her. As the junior officer, it was my job to sit at the head of the lower end of the table and, when the time came, to stand with a glass of port in my hand and say "Gentlemen," at which point all the other officers stood with their glasses at the ready and looked expectantly toward me. I then raised my glass and said the magic words, "The colonel of the regiment, Her Royal Highness Queen Elizabeth, the Queen Mother," whereupon everyone murmured "God bless her" before sipping their port and resuming their places. It was a ritual that many today would probably consider hilarious. I found it somewhat nerve-racking at first, thinking I might forget some of the words, but came to enjoy my role and to appreciate the many years of tradition behind it (our regiment was founded in 1688). I regarded this period of my military life as a kind of finishing school. But it soon came to an end.

One morning, along with two other junior officers, I was notified that I had been selected for service in Korea. We were to join the Middlesex Regiment, which had been there since the beginning of the war and had recently received heavy casualties. While some considered this tantamount to a death sentence, we were actually pleased to have been selected and wanted to get to the front as soon as possible. We were the generation that had just missed service in World War II, and we were anxious to "catch up" with our older brothers and their friends. In those days, one traveled by troopship, which meant a several-week journey before actually arriving in the war zone. Instead of being frustrating, this was a surprisingly pleasant experience. Our troopship was a converted ocean liner, the *Dunera*, and our month-long voyage was like a month's luxury cruise. As officers, we had first-class accommodations and service as we made our way through the Mediterranean, Suez Canal, Red Sea, Indian Ocean, and South China Sea, stopping at such exotic places as Port Said at the entrance to the Suez Canal, Aden (at the other end), Singapore, Colombo, and Hong Kong, and passing through the disputed Straits of Formosa before reaching our final destination of Kure in Japan, where we were greeted by a small military band on the quayside as we disembarked. It seemed quite anticlimactic.

However, we were just settling into our quarters in Kure when we were told to pack up and prepare for an emergency flight to Korea in the morning. I can still see our portly chaplain rushing around in a Red Cross ambulance to pick up extra supplies of ammunition. This was obviously serious. Early the next morning, our special train to the air base of Iwakuni passed slowly through Hiroshima, where the devastation of the atomic bomb five years earlier was still very apparent: not a building was standing. The few homes of survivors were made out of cardboard boxes. The whole scene was a terrible reminder of what Robert Burns called "man's inhumanity to man, that makes countless thousands mourn." One wondered what the future would hold.

We flew twice to Korea. The first time, our plane could not land because fighting was still raging around the airfield at Suwon, which was our destination. After circling the field for what seemed like ages, waiting for a green light to land, we returned to Japan. For most of us teenage soldiers this was the first time we had flown in a plane, and the endless circling and other aerial maneuvers made us all quite ill. The next day we were able to land, but were required to move on quickly. We boarded several army trucks that bounced us over heavily rutted roads and tracks before depositing us at a bedraggled encampment on the northern bank of the Han River, where we found the remains of the Middlesex Regiment. We had arrived. We received a warm enough welcome, though the Middlesex left us in no doubt that their number one desire was to get out of Korea as soon as possible. I asked how close the enemy were. "A mile or two up the road," I was told by a cheery Middlesex platoon commander. To my ears, that seemed fairly close. "Don't worry. You'll be seeing them tomorrow," he added. "We leave just before dawn."

"But it'll be dark."

"That's the point."

The Sharp End

We were now in a tactical area usually referred to by troops as the *sharp end*. Abandoned vehicles lay by the roadside. Then we came across the dead bodies, the stench from the decaying flesh making it almost impossible to breathe. We took up positions on the hills above the road, unsure of what to expect. But as so often, the enemy had left ahead of us, so we resumed our trek northward, remaining on the alert for sudden sniper fire or worse. At the end of the day, we dug new positions on a hill overlooking a broad valley and early the following morning began aggressive patrolling. The air still reeked of dead bodies. Over the next few months we spent much of our time patrolling, occupying new positions, and fighting occasional skirmishes with the enemy, who were also patrolling and were very silent and skillful about it. They were not North Koreans, but regular Chinese army units, who were far more sophisticated than any of us had anticipated. I learned that the reason we had been suddenly rushed to the front was that a carefully planned and executed Chinese attack had decimated Britain's Gloucester Regiment of about seven hundred men. This had been part of China's surprisingly successful spring offensive, which had eventually been halted just before I arrived. We were now slowly pushing the Chinese back toward the Imjin River and the thirty-eighth parallel that officially divided North and South Korea. Most of the fighting at this time was on one side or the other of that river, which wound lazily through quite beautiful, undulating countryside.

In August, the monsoon season in Korea, it was decided that we should start conducting long-range patrols deeper into enemy territory. I was assigned to lead one of them with about twenty men. We crossed the Imjin on pontoons and trekked warily toward high ground with good visibility of the Chinese frontline positions. Our orders were to hold our ground until further notice. As we arrived and started digging in, the wind strengthened and it began to rain, which quickly became very heavy. Soon we were in the middle of a full-fledged monsoon, unable to see more than a few yards in front of us. That night, the Imjin rose more than twenty feet by official count, sweeping away the pontoon bridges that were our lifeline to the rest of our forces, making it impossible to turn back or for reinforcements to move forward to join us. We were now thoroughly drenched. The foxholes we would have used to protect ourselves from attack were full to the brim of water and could not be bailed. We did all we could to keep our weapons dry, but it became virtually impossible. We realized all too well that we could not sustain a Chinese attack, but had to remain on total alert for the possibility.

After two days of isolation and mounting fears that an attack could come at any moment, the rain eased and—like a biblical dove—a single-person helicopter suddenly appeared and landed on our hill with food and other supplies. These small military helicopters were equipped with stretchers on each side of the cabin, so we were able to strap in our wounded before it left. The problem, of course, was that the helicopter immediately gave away our position. Our hope was that it would suggest to the Chinese that we were actually more numerous and better armed than the twenty or so soaking bodies they would have found had they attacked. The miracle was that they did not attack. On the third day, we were ordered to slowly make our way down the hill and back to the point where we had originally crossed the river, a distance of nearly three miles. Everyone was dead tired. We were still in Chinese-controlled territory, and I was very conscious of the fact that Chinese snipers were probably watching us every step of the way and could pick us off at any moment. I searched in vain for cover along the route in case we should need it. And I prayed. As it happened, the Chinese did not fire and we arrived safely at the riverbank. While all the pontoon bridges had been swept away by the now raging river, we were amazed to find that American army engineers had jury-rigged another way to cross the river, with small motorized vessels hitched to powerful overhead cables. We could not have been more impressed, or more grateful. When we got to the other side, to our surprise, we were greeted like heroes. I suspect that one reason for this was that the senior officers lined up to greet us were themselves more than a little relieved. They may have concluded that sending off lightly armed long-range patrols in the middle of the monsoon season was not, after all, a very smart idea.

The Middlesex Regiment was eventually rotated back to Hong Kong and replaced by the King's Shropshire Light Infantry, to which I was now attached since my national service time had not yet expired. About the same time, the various units from Commonwealth countries such as Australia, Britain, Canada, New Zealand, South Africa, and India were merged into a formal Commonwealth Division. In October 1951 the division was assigned the key role in a major new offensive, called Operation Commando, to capture several strategic hills immediately ahead. Chinese resistance turned out to be considerably greater than expected, and several units were unable to advance. The Australians were the exception, forging ahead of the rest of the division despite heavy casualties. They were by far the best-trained soldiers in the division and probably the best in the whole multinational United Nations force in Korea.

At this point, the relatively untested King's Shropshire Light Infantry was introduced to serious fighting for the first time. My own role was to lead an attack on a hill called 227, where a previous Allied attack had failed. Despite sporadic gunfire that cost us a few casualties on the way up, the enemy eventually fled. As we took possession, we were surprised to find the hill was in fact a mini-fortress, honeycombed with trenches and covered dugouts. The Chinese were obviously very good at digging such fortifications, and we felt quite luxurious as we settled into them, thinking that all the heavy lifting had already been done. We were expecting a long stay, but this was not to be.

Escape by Moonlight

After a couple of weeks of relative calm, the Chinese unleashed an artillery barrage against hill 227 that was described in the official history of the war as "heavier than anything ever experienced before—90 to 120 rounds per minute—*very heavy shelling by any standards.*" Trenches were pulverized, barbed wire was shattered, and our whole hill was on fire. When a shell exploded a few feet away from me, I became one of the casualties, with head and back shrapnel wounds. As I regained consciousness, I saw Chinese soldiers everywhere. My Sten gun was blocked by dirt and quite useless. A Chinese soldier, whom I took to be an officer, beckoned to me and directed me down the hill toward the Chinese lines. Looking around, I saw that about twenty more of our men had been given similar directions. We were technically prisoners—but, as it turned out, we were only loosely guarded. It was now dark, so we tried a maneuver that, if unsuccessful, could have resulted in our instant death from machine-gun fire. Instead of continuing down the hill, I led the group slowly in the opposite direction, through a minefield that we had laid some days before but that was now churned up by artillery fire. The trick was to carefully pick our way through without touching any of the mines, which were very difficult to see. I wasn't sure it could be done, given the darkness, but felt it was worth trying. None of us wanted to be a prisoner of the Chinese.

Our progress was painfully slow. But I found to my surprise that with sufficient focus on a small area, I could actually see quite well in the dark. Certainly we had the incentive. I periodically reminded those following me to step *exactly* in my footsteps and not to wander off on their own. I found myself thinking of King Wenceslas in the Christmas carol, "Mark my footsteps good my page, tread thou in them boldly." Talking was another problem. I had to constantly remind the men that even whispers could be heard a long way off by an attentive enemy. A few days later, the London *Daily Express* carried a front-page story on our escape. It began, "As the moon slipped behind a cloud, the whispered word went back ..." It was fun to read, and we wondered how they heard about us so quickly.

A silent, nail-biting hour after we began our trek, we emerged on the Allied side of the hill with only one casualty: someone had in fact stepped on a mine and totally shattered his leg. It was bad, but could have been much worse, and the wounded man was stoic in uttering no cry of pain or call for help in order not to give our position away. The nearest friendly positions were those of Princess Patricia's Canadian Light Infantry, on a hill on the other side of the valley. We made our way toward them. As we approached their barbed wire, our primary goal was to convince their sentries that we were on their side and there was no need to shoot. After some understandable hesitation, they seemed persuaded and let us through. I was able to use their radio to report in to my battalion headquarters, which asked if I was personally okay. I instinctively replied that I was, whereupon I was instructed to make my way back across the valley to take command of another platoon at the base of 227, whose officer had been killed. I did so and eventually fell asleep in a trench. When I awoke at first light my head was in a pool of blood from the wound

I had sustained, but had quite forgotten about. Fortunately, it did not require hospitalization, so I was able to take part in attempts over the next several days to regain control of 227 from the Chinese. Occupation of the hill went back and forth. The Chinese obviously felt it was an important piece of real estate in their plans to stop the Allied advance.

We were eventually withdrawn from the 227 area and sent to relieve the Royal Norfolk Regiment in positions to the west, overlooking the Samichon Valley near Panmunjom, where peace talks had begun. This was fairly peaceful by comparison (though later the scene of the last major battle of the war). We now had new territory to patrol, consisting largely of paddy fields, which, needless to say, did not offer much cover. Winter was setting in, and the frost-covered ground crunched noisily beneath our boots as we tried to maintain silence on our night patrols. The moon also was uncooperative—shining with what seemed unusually high intensity. We felt the Chinese could probably hear us and see us coming a mile away, so we were on constant alert for an ambush.

Christmas was now coming, and the Chinese had the annoying habit of hanging Christmas cards on the barbed wire in front of our positions. It was particularly alarming that they managed to crawl up to our positions overnight to hang the cards without any of our sentries noticing. But one couldn't help admiring their skill. The cards, too, were full of clever propaganda messages, full of good wishes, and hoping that we would soon be going home to be with our loved ones. They usually included a photo of President Truman in holiday garb on vacation in Key West, asserting that "he is on vacation—he doesn't care about you." We expected the cards and accompanying small gifts to be booby-trapped, but they weren't. Another example of quite sophisticated psychology on the part of the Chinese.

As my two years of military service were drawing to a close, I found to my surprise that I did not want to leave Korea. I felt I was involved in a campaign of considerable importance not just for the future of Korea, but also for the future of the civilized world. I thought it essential that our side should win and, in a small way, I could help make that happen, especially as I now had a year's combat experience behind me. I was now officially a veteran. I was physically very fit. I enjoyed the outdoor life (we were outdoors the whole time), enjoyed the comradeship of officers and men, and especially enjoyed the responsibility of commanding a platoon (thirty men) and sometimes, on a temporary basis, a company of four platoons. I was asked by my superior officers if I would be willing to extend my service by another six months and perhaps longer. I would have been overjoyed. But my elderly father was now seriously ill and I felt I might never see him again, so with a heavy heart I turned down the offer and began the formalities of disengagement ("sign this, sign that—where's the compass?"). Not much ceremony was involved in departing. I just picked up my old kitbag, caught a truck to the heavily damaged central station in Seoul, and then took a painfully slow, seven-hour cargo train ride to the southeastern port of Pusan, from which we were to sail.

The voyage home was considerably more subdued than our original voyage out. For one thing, we had been exposed to hundreds of dead and maimed bodies, including those of some of our own comrades, but also of untold numbers of Korean civilians. Korea was a broken country. Its once flourishing cities and towns and picturesque villages had been flattened. The only homes we could see were those made of cast-off cardboard boxes once used for American rations. The population of this proud, historic, and beautiful country was now living in total misery, surviving on food scraps and with virtually no shelter beyond a piece of cardboard to fend off the rain, with access to only the most rudimentary medical services. It was touching to see how closely parents watched after their children in these circumstances. Thousands of children, too, had become homeless orphans. I longed to join the United Nations to help rebuild the country, but felt that, not having a college degree, I probably would never have been accepted for much more than a clerk's job. Yet I clearly underestimated the resilience of the Korean people. It is still a miracle to me how the Korea I left in ruins and such deprivation became one of the great powerhouses of the modern world: a tribute not just to the resilience of the Korean people, but, surely, of all humanity. I could not imagine such a resurrection when I sadly boarded the troopship home.

It was now early 1952, and because of a periodic flare-up in our relations with Egypt, we did not stop at Port Said on the way home. Instead, we manned machine guns on the decks in case our ship was attacked by newly militant Egyptian troops. In the event, it wasn't. But in place of Egypt's Port Said, we stopped in Algiers, the beautiful French port city whose palm-lined streets and glistening white colonial buildings were framed by the sparkling blue of the Mediterranean. It was Paris-by-the-Sea.

The Daily Telegraph

Fleet Street Heaven

After being officially "demobilized," I returned to Hemel Hempstead and to the *Gazette*. This was no longer as exciting as it had seemed before I joined the army. The work was easy enough, but covering the local council and magistrates' courts and writing an occasional editorial on local matters (such as why the garbage is always collected at lunchtime) no longer had any appeal. I was bored and became cross with myself for getting short-tempered with colleagues and readers alike. For me, this was no longer the real world. It was clearly time to move on. I wrote to several of the London dailies, most of which did not reply, but one that did was *The Daily Telegraph*, which invited me to an interview with a gentlemanly assistant editor at its palatial white stone building at 135 Fleet Street. I bought a new suit for the occasion.

Fleet Street and its narrow side streets were the traditional home of British journalism, with rows of newspaper offices and news services, along with famous old restaurants and pubs where journalists met their contacts and often wrote their stories. Britain's first daily newspaper was published here around 1700, and Samuel Johnson wrote the first English dictionary at his home in Gough Square, just off Fleet Street, in the 1750s. For hundreds of years, this had been a famous community of writers and publishers, and it was the goal of every reporter to work here. A few days after my interview, I received a letter inviting me to join the *Telegraph*'s staff at the prevailing union wage of fourteen guineas a week (about sixty dollars at the time). I was in heaven.

At twenty, I was by far the youngest member of the reporting staff. Since I had only recently completed my military service, I believe that my stint in Korea appealed to the paper's conservative management. Otherwise, the editorial staff tended to be above average in age, mostly veterans of World War II and some even of World War I. The newsroom felt very much like an officers' mess— quiet, polite, dignified. These qualities were also reflected in the paper's reporting. We were the biggest of the nation's serious papers and the most popular with the establishment—military officers, politicians, and the clergy. The *Telegraph* sold over a million copies a day—four times more than *The Times* or any other serious daily.

Our billboards proclaimed that we were "Readable, Reliable, Realistic." All of which was true. We were by far the best paper in the country—in fact, with *The New York Times*, one of the two best papers in the world. We had the best reporters, best foreign correspondents, best editors, and best management. We also had the best owners—the Welsh Camrose family, who spent whatever it took for the *Telegraph* to remain at the top. I did not fully realize how privileged I was to be there in my early twenties, with nationally known colleagues such as Bill Deedes (later a cabinet minister) and Malcolm Muggeridge (later editor of the humor magazine *Punch* and a noted BBC personality). It was an incredible hands-on experience for a young man learning the craft of journalism.

The first thing I noticed about working for a daily paper, as opposed to a weekly, was that you do not have to work quite so many hours. The paper has enough staff and is required to respect union rules, so you are not expected to put in more than seven or eight hours a day or five days a week. This was new to me—so much so that during my first week I turned up on Saturday morning expecting a full day's work, only to be told to go home.

My first modest reporting assignment for the *Telegraph* was to cover a historical exhibit of hearing aids, in a building just off Trafalgar Square, the square dedicated to Admiral Lord Nelson, hero of the famous Battle of Trafalgar. The organizers insisted I talk with the chairman of the event, Lord Nelson. Lord Nelson? It was well known that the famous admiral had no sons, but the title had percolated down through various cousins to the sixth Earl Nelson, whom I found myself interviewing on this morning about Victorian ear trumpets. Though he was from a distinguished naval family, it turned out he was not a sailor but a lecturer in anthropology. I used to pride myself on being able to find a story in everyone, but, try as I might, I could not find a story good enough for the *Telegraph* in either the event or his lordship. Our news editor, a wonderful Scotsman named Alex McLaren, was sympathetic. Apparently they hadn't expected anything. He told me to write a brief paragraph for the society column.

Fog in Highgate!

I was soon promoted to writing the day's weather story. Though this was simple enough, based largely on wire service copy, I soon learned that the *Telegraph*'s weather stories had certain characteristics that set them apart. One of them was making sure we covered weather conditions in the areas where our more upscale readers lived. Highgate was a typical example. It was one of the oldest, wealthiest, and most charming of suburbs, bordering Hampstead Heath and high enough above sea level that it provided views of most of London. But the most important reason we covered it was that many leaders of London society—politicians, actors, writers—lived there. Among them was one of our senior assistant editors, who upon arriving home in the evening would call in to the newsroom to let us know the current weather conditions in Highgate. I remember the first call I took from him, letting me know that "there's fog in Highgate." In those days, there was almost always fog somewhere, and I didn't immediately realize the import of including in our national weather story the fact that there was fog in Highgate. *Why,* I thought, *should anyone care?* One of the senior reporters on the night shift enlightened me. Unlike other papers, the *Telegraph did* care.

Another staple of our weather stories was including the 10 p.m. temperature in central London. The location everyone used for this was the weather station on the roof of the Air Ministry. The night press officer at the ministry was usually waiting for our call, which was probably the highlight of his evening shift. Our weather stories were written earlier, but left space for this last-minute addition, which by now had become something of a ritual. One evening, as the clock ticked away—it was now about 9:45—the night editor, harassed by a number of stories all breaking at the same time, saw me sitting quietly at my desk and asked if I had the ten o'clock temperature yet. No, I replied, glancing at the newsroom clock, I was waiting for ten o'clock. Visibly irritated, he replied, "Well you can *try*, can't you?"

In fact, I did try once or twice to get an early read on the night's temperature, but found that the Air Ministry official in question did not himself go up to the roof to check the instruments until ten o'clock, and did not appreciate being rushed.

"The Glorious Twelfth"

I have always remembered August 11th. It is the day before the grouse shooting season begins in the United Kingdom, referred to by aficionados as "the glorious twelfth." It is an important day not only for British sportsmen, but also for sportsmen all over the world who each year flock to Scotland and parts of northern England and Ireland for the opening of the season—comparable in a way to Royal Ascot, the Henley Regatta, and other traditional sporting events for the upper classes. It came into my life on this particular August 11ᵗʰ in the voice of our news editor. "Adams," he boomed, "we need half a column on the opening of the grouse shooting season." I was not quite sure what a grouse was, nor where to begin in writing about the opening of the season. The news editor must have been amused by the expression on my face. "Go to the library," he instructed, "and see what we wrote last year." So I did, and quickly brushed up on the terminology of the moors and the beaters and the fact that the best grouse were red. More importantly, last year's story contained the names of various dukes and earls on whose land the grouse nested and who typically hosted large parties for the beginning of the season. I called them up and chatted with them about the prospects for the coming season and how it compared with last year, doing my best to sound as if I knew what I was talking about. I got my half column.

Although we were one of the very few papers that covered this event, I was impressed by the fact that it existed at all (and still does, having grown in importance over the years because of its contributions to the British economy). I learned that it is an almost entirely British phenomenon, due to the unique peculiarities of the climate and the northern vegetation. But what amazed me most about this whole story was the level of coordination on the day the season began. Apparently the first grouse on the twelfth were always rushed to London Airport and flown to New York, where they were met at the airport by a special courier who whisked them across Manhattan to the famous 21 Club, where they were served as a delicacy on that evening's menu.

The Death Watch

All new reporters were required to take their turn at writing obituaries. This could be more interesting than it sounds. For one thing, it was an area in which we competed head-to-head with *The Times*, whose obituaries were legendary for their length and detail. While some obituaries were based on wire service stories, others were discovered in the day's death notices, provided to us at the end of the business day by the paper's advertising department. Our job was to check them all for possible previous references in our library's extensive files, known as the morgue, as well as with *Who's Who*, *Debrett's Peerage*, and, for European notables, the *Almanac de Gotha*.

One evening I wrote a fairly short obit about a professor of radio astronomy at Cambridge University who, according to the death notice, had died suddenly in his forties. But at about ten o'clock the night news editor came up to my desk—I can still see his hands quivering—and asked if I was sure I had "buried" the right man, whereupon he showed me the early edition of the next day's *Times*, which carried a full-page obit of the *father* of the man I had written about. In an amazing coincidence, they both were radio astronomers at Cambridge and had exactly the same name. The father, however, was in his eighties and was far more famous, so the copy editors all assumed the *Times* was right and that I, a novice at the obituary game, must have made a terrible error. I checked my notes, based on the information I had, but now was feeling very nervous. I felt sure I would be fired for making such a huge mistake. "There is only one thing to do," the night editor said. "Call the home and ask them"

It was now nearly eleven o'clock at night, and I hesitated to bother the family on such a sad day, but I was in no position to argue. Our presses were about to roll. I found the home phone number and called. The widow of the younger man answered the phone and confirmed that it was her husband who had died, not his father. Despite my genuine sympathy and apologies, she then spent several minutes telling me how the *Telegraph* should be ashamed of itself for calling the home so late at night. But her anger was nothing compared with my feeling of relief. I wondered how the *Times* would handle its quite colossal mistake. The next day, it carried a lengthy obit of the younger man, preceding it with a note saying that his father, whose obit they had carried the previous day, "happily, is still with us." I couldn't help wondering how the widow felt.

The *Telegraph* had a policy of always carrying obituaries of people with titles, however insignificant their lives. Many were sons or daughters of famous people, but had done nothing very much themselves. Many, too, were retired colonial administrators or public health officials with minor titles, but I found these quite fascinating as I traced their lives and various promotions. I used to wonder what it must have been like as a magistrate, doctor, or postmaster in the lesser-known regions of India and Africa where even road travel was virtually impossible. It seemed to me that their titles, however minor, had been earned the hard way.

Every now and then we would have a suicide, but I quickly learned that we never used that word, presumably because the coroner had not yet ruled on the matter. Thus the person in question had always "died suddenly."

London has always had more than its fair share of eccentrics. One day I noticed a traditional black taxicab wending its way down Fleet Street, but its sides were covered in wickerwork, as if the cab had been placed in a huge wicker basket. When I expressed my surprise to a colleague, he explained, "Oh, that's old Gulbenkian. He's the richest man in the world, but doesn't like to show it." I did not know that I would soon be writing the obit of Calouste Gulbenkian. He was popularly known as "Mr. Five Percent" because he took 5 percent of every deal he arranged. No more, no less. These were huge international deals, mostly in the oil industry. For example, he was involved in arranging the merger that became Royal Dutch/Shell and became a 5 percent shareholder. At one time, too, he had title to all the oil in Iraq, but kept only 5 percent. "Better a small piece of a big pie than a big piece of a small one," he said in explaining his philosophy. His formula certainly worked. At the time of his death in 1955 his fortune was estimated at nearly a billion dollars (more than $10 billion today) and he owned one of the world's greatest private art collections. He gave away millions to charity and artistic and scientific causes, and reserved at least a half billion dollars to restore an ancient cathedral in his native Armenia.

Saving a Roman Temple

One of the advantages of being on the obit shift, which began at three in the afternoon, was that I had the rest of the day to explore London at my leisure. I focused mostly on the old city of London, which was being slowly rebuilt after heavy German bombing during World War II. I wrote several pieces about the restoration of Wren churches for the paper's upscale diary column called "London Day by Day." These were perfect for our conservative readership, and I gained something of a reputation within the paper for my efforts. Nobody else, at our paper or others, was covering this "soft" beat. It was during my wanderings around the city's ruins that I came across the biggest story of my life. As I looked through a wooden fence surrounding a site scheduled for development, I could see a couple of people standing in a puddle at the bottom of the site who were obviously not workers. I found a way through the fence and scrambled down the hill to ask them what they were doing there, thinking they might be architects. It turned out they were archaeologists. They explained that they had discovered the outline of a Roman temple and were finding some extremely well-preserved artifacts, but unfortunately would have to give up their work the following day because the bulldozers were scheduled to start work excavating the site for a major office building. The office building, called Bucklesbury House, would be by far the biggest built in the city since World War II, and the archaeologists' appeals for more time had been turned down because it would cost too much to keep the bulldozers and other contractors waiting.

What a story! This was not only about bulldozing a just-discovered Roman temple in the heart of London, but the temple appeared to be dedicated to the god Mithras, known to have been worshipped by Roman soldiers. According to the archaeologists, this was especially important as no other temple to Mithras had ever been found in England. The chief archaeologist involved, William Grimes, was director of the London Museum and obviously a trustworthy source. I did not need to seek confirmation from anyone else. I dashed back to the office and wrote my story. This was a Thursday. The story appeared on Friday. On Saturday and Sunday, thousands of protesters from all over Britain descended on the site with placards demanding "Stop the Bulldozers!" Winston Churchill was still prime minister, and members of Parliament called on him to take immediate action to "stop this sacrilege." He promised to talk to the developers, who agreed to wait another month so that the archaeologists could complete their work.

According to Wikipedia, this was "perhaps the most famous of all twentieth-century Roman discoveries in the City of London."

The site was close to Liverpool Street Station, a major commuter hub for city office workers, who before boarding their trains home began to line up, sometimes for hours, for the opportunity to view the remains of the temple. To accommodate them, the archaeologists took the major artifacts as they were found—typically vases and sculptured heads of gods and goddesses, including the head of Mithras himself—and walked up the hill and along the lines of office workers to show and explain them. This went on for days. It became what today we would call a *happening*. A huge social and educational gathering, it was the top news of the day, day after day.

The temple foundations were eventually moved to another location in nearby Queen Victoria Street, where they were reassembled for display to the public and remain so to this day. Ironically, there is now talk of demolishing Bucklesbury House and returning the temple of Mithras to its original site.

A few months later, a book on the whole event was published by the archaeological correspondent of the *Times*, who had totally missed the original story. *What hubris*, I thought. Then I blamed myself for not thinking of doing the same thing. Dr. Grimes and others also wrote books about it. It was obviously a much more significant event than I realized at the time. Like most people, probably including the prime minister, I had never previously heard of Mithras.

The British have long had a reputation for understatement. This was certainly the case at the *Telegraph*. A classic example was the reaction of the owners and top editors to my story about the temple. Whereas American editors would probably say "great" and "attaboy" or at least "congratulations," a brief memo came down from the top floor to the news editor as follows:

> From Mr. Stowell
> To Mr. McLaren
>
> Adams's story on the Roman finds in London was liked, but he should have explained the rather rare phrase "opus signinum floor."

Perhaps needless to say, I have never had another occasion to use that "rather rare phrase."

Sherry with the Duke

and other sobering moments

Because of my still fairly recent army service, the *Telegraph*'s news editors tended to give me any odd stories involving the military. We had an official military correspondent, a retired lieutenant general named H. G. Martin, but he dealt chiefly with analyzing developments at the policy level. We seldom saw him in the newsroom. (Initials in bylines were common at the time. My byline was A. J. B. Adams.)

One policy issue I did become involved with was the planned acquisition of the new Belgian FN rifle, which was due to be adopted by NATO. I read that the senior civil servant in the Ministry of Supply, responsible for the purchase of weapons, was retiring from the government to take a position with the company manufacturing the FN. This did not sound right to me. I wasn't sure what I could do about it, until I learned that some friends of mine in the Royal Marines had been given responsibility for testing the weapon. I got in touch with them and asked how the testing was coming along. Not well, they told me. In particular, the FN was subject to numerous stoppages for which there was no obvious explanation. I pressed for more details, and they were readily forthcoming. In short, this vaunted new weapon, developed at great cost to taxpayers, was proving to be a bust.

I was especially sensitive to stoppages, since the ancient Sten and Bren guns we had used in Korea were easily stopped by sand entering the breach, and this had been a major problem when exploding artillery shells kicked up dirt all over infantry positions. I had personally experienced this and knew it could lead to countless unnecessary deaths and other casualties. So although reporters are not supposed to become advocates, I effectively became one. I felt I knew enough about the operational side of this matter to do my best to make sure the problem with the FN was fixed before the weapon was widely adopted and issued to troops in the field. The marines agreed with me, resulting in a front-page story in the *Telegraph* noting the weapon's numerous flaws. The War Office (Defense Department) and Ministry of Supply were not amused and complained mightily to the owner and top editors of the paper, who, I am proud to say, stood by me. General Martin would never have written such a story.

One of my quasi-military assignments was to take the train to Ascot each Sunday—not for the races, but for the famous rifle range at Bisley next door. The *Telegraph* traditionally carried the results of the main shooting events. Though essentially a rather routine assignment, one day while I was there a bullet ricocheted off the target and hit a butt marker (a person who stands in a trench below the target to signal where the bullet hit), who had to be rushed to the hospital. This had never been known to happen before, and I was able to get the head of Bisley to say it was a million-in-one chance. This was enough for a story on the front page of the *Telegraph*'s Monday edition—the first time that anything about Bisley had appeared on the front page.

Around this time I received an unexpected compliment from the editors of the editorial page, who asked me to write a short op-ed, with my byline, on how Bisley was coping with the FN and other less-traditional firearms. It was easy enough to do, and it certainly raised my profile both inside and outside the paper, since in those days the *Telegraph* did not give bylines to newsroom reporters, only to foreign correspondents. Shortly thereafter, I was asked to research and write a series on the impoverished state of housing for military families. I traveled the country visiting various facilities, including Eaton Hall, the officer cadet school from which I had graduated not too long ago, but which had recently experienced a series of suicides. It was an odd feeling inspecting the place where I had so recently trained. As it happened, the place appeared to be considerably safer and more luxurious than in my day—and I could find no reason for the rash of suicides.

My tour of military housing was not very exciting, but it ended perfectly. My last visit was to the Royal Horse Guards barracks in Aldershot, just outside London, where I arrived just before lunch. The duty officer invited me into the officers' mess for a drink and to meet their commanding officer, the Duke of Wellington. I thought he was pulling my leg, but he assured me that the current duke (the eighth) was indeed their commanding officer. At that time, the Irish Republican Army in Britain was conducting a campaign to steal weapons and ammunition from military facilities by overpowering the traditionally unarmed guards and breaking into the armories. There was much debate in Parliament and the media over how to deal with this outbreak. The big question was whether the guards should be armed, the concern being that nervous young guards might accidentally kill someone. So here I was chatting over sherry with the Duke of Wellington, whose illustrious ancestor had defeated Napoleon at Waterloo. I asked him how he was handling the question of arming the guards. He was immediately forthcoming, telling me that his policy was to have the guards armed, but with only one bullet "up the spout." In other words, they could get off only one shot—enough to alert the regiment and scare away the would-be robbers.

For a reporter, this was manna from heaven. Regardless of the efficacy of the duke's plan, for the military-oriented *Telegraph*, an exclusive interview with the Duke of Wellington on the hot military topic of the day could certainly be considered a coup, and it was perfect for the paper's popular political column, "London Day by Day," which Bill Deedes edited and *everybody* read. I had called the story in from a public phone box and went home. There were no cell phones in those days, so it wasn't until the following morning that I saw whether they had used it. I was happy to see that it was the lead item of the column.

With my visits to military housing over, I was asked to write the leading op-ed for the editorial page to put the whole issue in perspective, with my name in relatively large letters at the top. I was now twenty-three years old and felt I was on my way—but was not quite sure where it was leading. I desperately wanted to get abroad, to become a bona fide foreign correspondent. Most of all, I wanted to be the first Western correspondent reporting from *inside* Communist China. Failing that, I wanted the paper to send me to East Africa to report on the British troops fighting there. To no avail. This was 1956. With a few months' patience, I could have been sent to cover the revolution in Hungary or the Suez Canal war, both of which broke out in October of that year. But patience, it seems, was not one of my strong suits.

No. 1 Place Vendome was one of the more fashionable addresses in Paris, a period townhouse whose elaborate chandeliers, floor-to-ceiling windows, and gilded mirrors suggested it was still the residence of one of France's great families, but in fact it was the Paris bureau of *The Daily Telegraph*, and it was where I longed to work. The Ritz hotel was just across the street. My French grandfather, Antoine Bertrand, a noted chef in Paris and London, had known César Ritz, so I felt this was truly the place where I belonged. Paris was the oldest and at that time the most important of the *Telegraph*'s foreign bureaus, with responsibility for covering developments in French North Africa and the Middle East, as well as the kaleidoscopic politics of France itself.

Two seasoned correspondents, John Wallis and Jeffrey Myers, had a firm grip on the Paris bureau, but were periodically supported by younger reporters on loan from the London office. I applied for a two-month leave and took myself to Paris. My immediate goal was to convince Wallis, the bureau chief, that I should be one of the reporters he asked for. Aside from showing me how to drink my first-ever Pernod at his local bar, he was not particularly encouraging. The third person in the Paris bureau was a much-coveted slot, he explained, and usually went to someone with special connections. The current third person, for example, was John Herbert, son of the playwright A. P. Herbert, who was wealthy, charming, and well known in society. I did not want to be a nuisance, but asked if they would accept an occasional story from me while I was there anyway. They agreed they would look at anything I wrote, but it was clear they did not expect me to come up with anything of interest.

I enrolled for French history and literature classes at the Alliance Française, and got a cheap room with students from all over the world at an amazing housing complex called the Cité Universitaire on the outskirts of town. This, I thought, gave me an edge. I was sure no one at the Paris bureau had ever set foot in the Cité. It was not a *Telegraph* kind of place. But the paper did have an interest in French food, and the prices in the Cité's cavernous cafeteria were so ridiculously low by any standard that I wrote a piece about the place and its food for the *Telegraph*'s popular "Letter from Paris." To my great delight, they used it. But I shouldn't get my hopes up, they cautioned; it could be years before I could get a posting to the Paris bureau. I returned to London and started thinking about other possibilities for a foreign assignment.

The opportunity came not from the *Telegraph* but from a small classified ad in a trade paper, the *World's Press News*. An unnamed news organization "on the continent" was seeking a copy editor. I applied. The organization turned out to be Radio Free Europe, and the location was Munich. I found this disappointing, since I had my heart set on Paris, and the very name Munich had such ominous overtones. I had very little interest in working in Germany, which, to me, was still enemy territory. I had never heard of Radio Free Europe, but was somewhat intrigued by its name, so I checked with David Floyd, our Communist-affairs correspondent, to see what he knew about it—and especially, whether it might just be a fly-by-night operation. I knew how lucky I was to be at the *Telegraph* and didn't want to give it up for anything too risky. He assured me that it was a sound organization, supported by President Eisenhower and the American Congress, and encouraged me to pursue the opportunity. This is how I came to spend the next seven years in Germany.

Radio Free Europe

The Struggle for Freedom

Radio Free Europe was an American weapon in the Cold War—an extremely effective weapon, which many credit with making a major contribution to the ultimate defeat of the Soviet Union. Having recently fought against the North Korean and Chinese armies in Korea, I felt comfortable enough with the radio's mission, which was to break through the communists' propaganda apparatus to bring straight news and analysis to the people behind the Iron Curtain, in their own languages—the kind of service they would receive from their own stations if they were free and independent nations instead of satellites of the Soviet Union.

Radio Free Europe was an impressive organization—physically and intellectually. It occupied a huge, rambling two-story building on the edge of Munich's largest park. It had been designed with especially wide corridors so that it could eventually be converted to a hospital. It was full of broadcast studios, radio monitoring operations, briefing rooms, newsrooms, and editorial offices. It also had shortwave broadcasting facilities elsewhere in Germany and in

Portugal, from where the broadcasts were bounced off the ionosphere to overcome communist jamming. Radio Free Europe had a staff of more than a thousand multilingual writers, broadcasters, and engineers from the countries we were broadcasting to (Poland, Hungary, Czechoslovakia, Bulgaria, and Rumania), as well as topflight German and American technicians and a relatively small number of American supervisors and intelligence experts. It was a truly vibrant environment.

Beyond the radio's headquarters in Munich, we had a dozen news bureaus all over Europe. Each was headed by a veteran American or British correspondent with deep European experience, such as Eric Gedye in Vienna, Allan Michie in London, Russell Hill in Berlin, and Allan Dreyfuss in Paris. The bureau reporters were all émigré, who interviewed escapees, authors, politicians, and reporters just back from reporting trips to Eastern Europe. My first assignment after joining RFE was to edit translations of the often dramatic reports from these bureaus. It felt as if we were in a war, and we were—an ideological war fought over the airwaves. Our first-class monitoring facilities were key. We closely monitored everything the East European governments were telling their listeners, and each morning the national desk chiefs met with our American political advisers and other experts to dissect what the communists were saying and decide how best to respond.

The year 1956—when I joined RFE—was the height of the Cold War, providing RFE and the West in general with a series of dramatic challenges. It began with Soviet premier Khrushchev's "secret speech" in which he denounced Stalin and his immediate circle as criminals (Stalin had died in 1953) and ended with the Hungarian Revolution, the climactic and bloodiest event of the Cold War, for which the West was ill prepared and RFE was subsequently and unfairly blamed.

This was all far more demanding and emotionally draining than I had ever anticipated when I innocently responded to that blind ad for a copy editor. Radio Free Europe itself was in a state of high drama, unable to predict the outcome in Hungary and fearful that the revolution might spread to Poland and potentially lead to a third world war. Everyone was tense. Arguments flew, both externally and internally. The Hungarian desk, headed by a charming former diplomat named Istvan Bede, was overwhelmed. The U.S. State Department was sending daily "guidance" from afar, with which our political advisers frequently disagreed—at the risk of their careers. Our monitoring operations were picking up radio messages around the clock from hastily formed student and worker "councils" all over Hungary. These were often heartrending, begging for help from the West. Our Hungarian researchers also worked around the clock to provide essential background and biographical information for the other desks, and ultimately for Washington. Soviet tanks rolled into Budapest, and then rolled out again as even the Soviet Union was unsure how to respond, and then rolled in again as it became clear that neither the United States nor the United Nations was going to take any action.

The revolution began October 23 with high hopes for liberation and ended tragically on November 4, as Soviet tanks restored "order." More than 2,500 Hungarians—many of them students— were killed in the fighting. Some 200,000 escaped to the West. By January 1957, all opposition had been suppressed.

Many books have been written on the revolution, as well as on the role of Radio Free Europe. Its younger sister station, Radio Liberty, broadcast to the various republics of the Soviet Union, such as Latvia, Lithuania, and Georgia. The two organizations were eventually merged and continue to this day as RFE/RL. As the countries of Eastern Europe became free, RFE/RL refocused its broadcasting to other countries where freedom of the press was still virtually unknown, such as Afghanistan, Iraq, and Iran, as well as to Russia itself, whose brief burst of press freedom under Boris Yeltsin was quickly squelched by Vladimir Putin. Today, some sixty years after it was launched, RFE/RL still broadcasts in twenty-eight languages to twenty-one countries. So much for my concerns that it might be a fly-by-night organization.

The communist governments of Eastern Europe did all they could to block our broadcasts through jamming, designed to make our programs very difficult to hear, and they routinely arrested anyone or any family caught listening. Luckily, our superior American technology was largely able to overcome the jamming. But the communist governments and intelligence services also resorted to other forms of intimidation and sabotage, ranging from the relatively amateurish scattering of spikes in the parking lots to shred employees' tires to poisoning the salt shakers in the RFE cafeteria, to capturing and sometimes murdering individual broadcasters. Somehow they managed to poison the office coffee of RFE director Erik Hazelhoff with atropine, laying him low for several days and causing his eventual hospitalization, and they clumsily sought to capture the chief of the Polish desk, Jan Nowak, while he was on a reporting trip to Stockholm. Then in 1981, they hired an international terrorist gang to successfully blow up one of the wings of the RFE building, causing more than a hundred casualties. (More recently, RFE/RL reporters have been among the many journalists murdered in Russia.) We were definitely in a war. The increasingly desperate efforts to stop us were seen as evidence of our success in penetrating what Churchill famously called the Iron Curtain. They also were regarded as evidence of the communist governments' recognition of their own shaky hold on power.

Our goal as broadcasters was not to foment revolution, but to keep the East European populations—particularly the opinion leaders—well informed of developments in the world outside their borders and to help them maintain their national culture despite all Soviet efforts to destroy it. Thus we had programs devoted to their history, music, and art, as well as sports. We covered their teams at the Olympic Games more thoroughly than their national broadcasts did. Our broadcasters' names became favorites with listeners, though often they were not their real names, for fear of retribution against their families and friends in their home countries. Jan Nowak, for instance, continued to use his wartime code name, though his real name was Zdzislaw Jezioranski.

The top editors and broadcasters of RFE were people of great character and experience, who before escaping to the West had been leaders in many walks of life—political and labor leaders, diplomats, academics, economists, journalists and authors, military officers, and in many cases leaders of the anti-Nazi or anti-communist underground. Several were survivors of Hitler's concentration camps. Many—perhaps most—had lost all their relatives and all material possessions. They had lived through some of the most brutal political upheavals in history. Listening to their stories was, for me, a tremendous education. It was all very different from the relatively peaceful and disengaged suburbia of my own background, and where so many of today's journalists spend their relatively comfortable lives.

While I developed great respect for all my RFE colleagues, three were born leaders—men of the greatest integrity and influence who, for me, embodied the very spirit of RFE's mission of bringing freedom and democracy to the Soviet-occupied countries of Eastern Europe. The most prominent of these was Jan Nowak, who headed the radio's Polish operation—by far the station's largest and most successful. During World War II he had been a courier between the Polish underground in Warsaw (the Home Army) and the Polish government in exile in London. He would be parachuted into German-occupied Poland at night, carrying messages from the exile government. After strategy discussions with the leaders of the underground, he would make his way back to London in various disguises, often as a Swedish merchant sailor, to brief the Polish and British authorities on the latest Nazi activities. He was in Warsaw for the uprising in 1944, manning a clandestine radio, before escaping to Sweden. He was the first to reach the West with news of the destruction of the Warsaw Ghetto. After the war he served with the

Polish service of the BBC until he was recruited by the Americans to create and lead the Polish service of RFE.

Although not trained as a journalist, Nowak had perfect instincts for the job, and thoroughly understood the importance of symbolism. He thus insisted that the first broadcast of RFE's Polish service should be on Poland's national day of independence. And to demonstrate that this was truly a surrogate domestic service, the very first news item was that day's weather forecast for different parts of Poland. No other foreign broadcasting service got into this much detail, or was equipped to provide it. Radio Free Europe showed from the start that it was going to be deeply involved. Polish audiences loved it, and the communist authorities were shaken. They did everything they could to block the broadcasts, arrest anyone caught listening, and attack and undermine the staff of RFE's Polish desk.

Already a Polish hero, Nowak went on to direct the Polish service for the next twenty-five often turbulent years, during which he developed a huge following for his patriotic but levelheaded commentaries. The Polish Solidarity leader and later president, Lech Walesa, gave much credit to the RFE Polish service for the eventual overthrow of that country's communist government, which led in rapid succession to the overthrow of other communist regimes throughout Eastern Europe and the eventual demise of the Soviet Union. In retirement, Nowak wrote of his wartime experiences in the book *Courier from Warsaw*, which became a best seller in Poland and among Poles living in America and around the world. He also became an adviser on Poland and Eastern Europe to several American presidents, congressmen, and secretaries of state. He played a major role in bringing Poland into NATO and the European Union before his death in Warsaw at age ninety-one after a full life devoted to his country's interests. His wife, a true heroine of the Polish resistance, had predeceased him. They had no children.

Another important figure during my time at RFE was Erik Hazelhoff, head of the European operations of RFE. He was a

Dutch war hero who flew with the RAF's elite Pathfinder Force, piloting lightweight Mosquito fighter-bombers to illuminate targets over Germany for Allied heavy bombers. He was awarded the Distinguished Flying Cross in addition to numerous Dutch awards and in 1945 was appointed an equerry to Queen Wilhelmina. After the war, he went into broadcasting in the United States, becoming a vice president of NBC before being recruited as director of RFE in Munich at the beginning of 1956. He was a charismatic leader and did much to hold the various sectors of RFE together during the many serious challenges of that year. He and Nowak, two war veterans who had played important roles in their countries' respective underground movements, understood and respected each other. Both were fighters. One of their biggest burdens was dealing with the constant second-guessing from RFE's official headquarters in New York and the U.S. State Department and various members of Congress in Washington, who lived in a different world. Thankfully, they were up to the task. Hazelhoff later gained fame for writing of his wartime experiences in the book *Soldier of Orange*, which was also made into an award-winning movie.

The third member of this leadership troika was William E. Griffith, one of the world's foremost experts on communism, who was chief political adviser to RFE from its outset in 1950 through 1958. He was a genuine intellectual with a sparkling wit, whose knowledge and personality were perfect for the task of leading so many different nationalities—and egos—through the height of the Cold War. In my view, these three men embodied all that was good, courageous, and often inspiring about RFE and the American commitment to defeating communism in Europe, making it a true privilege to be part of their team.

As for me, my work changed quite rapidly. After the Hungarian Revolution I was promoted in quick succession to chief editor, chief of research and evaluation, and then to acting head of the three-hundred-person news and information division, in charge of our internal news operation as well as the news bureaus in twelve countries. I found that I enjoyed managing. I also discovered that the secret of successful management was a competent secretary. I was lucky enough to have three—all handsome American women at the top of their game. I was eventually informed that I could not go beyond "acting" chief of any of these units, because I was not an American citizen. Radio Free Europe was extremely security conscious, for good reason. Attempts were constantly being made to infiltrate our operations, many of them successful. I should have been the least of their worries. But all turned out well. I was sent to Bonn, the West German capital, to open RFE's first bureau there and become, at last, a bona fide foreign correspondent. I was also to act as liaison with the German government, which was officially supportive of RFE but was under constant political pressure from the Sudeten Germans and other right-wing expellee groups to close down the broadcasts.

Before leaving Munich, I had the pleasure of hosting a dinner for Griffith and some of his colleagues with Kingsley Martin, the influential editor of Britain's leading left-wing opinion weekly, the *New Statesman*. Martin was in Munich for a lecture and was happy to meet with the RFE people. He was interested in RFE, though not overly sympathetic. Before leaving London I had met with him to see if there might be an opportunity for submitting occasional pieces from Munich. I had not yet done so (we were essentially in different worlds), but I liked him. He had an endearing rumpled quality typical of so many top editors and writers. I felt like an Oxford don as I presided over a stimulating dinner conversation about RFE, communism, Europe, the United States, and the future of the world. I was happy to be in such company and hoped it would be good for RFE's image with the British press.

Though I didn't write for the *New Statesman*, I did continue to write occasional pieces for the *Telegraph*, including a story in the first issue of the new *Sunday Telegraph* on how Bulgarian refugees, in interviews, had expressed preference for a form of British constitutional monarchy. Perfect for the *Telegraph*. I also wrote for a conservative political weekly called *Truth*. Though it had a much smaller circulation and less influence than the *New Statesman*, it had some distinguished writers, including the leading British playwright J. B. Priestley, and a young music critic named Bernard Levin, whom I came to know. Levin went on to a brilliant career as a political columnist for *The Times*.

Balloon Diplomacy

One of the stories I wrote for *Truth* was about a little-known operation allied with RFE called the Free Europe Press, which specialized in developing written material for distribution in Hungary, Poland, and Czechoslovakia—mostly leaflets, but also miniature newspapers and even books, such as Arthur Koestler's famous anti-totalitarian *Darkness at Noon*, usually written by democratic refugees from those countries, now living in the West. What intrigued me was the method of distribution—they were sent by balloon from "secret locations" in Germany. I requested permission to visit one of these locations to see how the operation worked. Following are excerpts from my story:

> The balloon station, seventeen miles from the Czech border, was set among hills two thousand feet up outside the small Bavarian town of Freyung. We arrived at dusk. After a four-hour drive east from Munich we left the road and lurched up a farm track, following "FEP" arrows, half concealed and mud-bespattered like military TAC-signs, until the balloon station emerged in front of us. It looked uncomfortably like a POW camp. Arc-lights played on the formidable wire fences, and a familiar watch-tower overlooked the group of wooden buildings within. A uniformed guard, with FEP on his cap, examined our papers, and police dogs growled in the background.

"We'll be starting in a few minutes," the site manager announced, leading me into the packing hall in one of the huts. It was a hive of activity. About twenty men were preparing loads for the three thousand or so balloons to be launched that night. The main production line was a double-tier bench running down the center of the room, on either side of which a dozen men were rapidly tying up bundles of miniature newspapers. To each bundle they attached a wire contraption, about a foot long, called a double-trigger-action release mechanism. This, at the appropriate time, would set the newspapers free.

In a corner three men were hammering away at blocks of ice, and close to them a couple carefully weighed the pieces on small scales and popped them into brown paper envelopes. The weight varied with each flight, depending on the meteorologists' calculations at FEP headquarters in Munich. This evening, 150 grams of dry ice was being placed in each envelope. I felt I must be standing in what *Reader's Digest* might describe as the world's most amazing publishing department.

The production hall was a high wooden building resembling an army gymnasium, but in place of wall bars it had twenty-two gas pipes projecting at shoulder height from the walls. These were the inflation stations. Next to each pipe lay a lifeless heap of uninflated balloons, huge silver cocoons. The German operators, one to each station, placed the first balloons on the gas nozzles and attached the dropping devices, newspaper bundles, and packets of ice. Hoses led from the pipes to the hydrogen cylinders outside. There was then the sort of lull you get before a newspaper press roars into action. Then the site manager blew on a horn, the hoses gave a wiggle, and twenty-two balloons on pipes hissed and billowed up to a height of about ten feet each.

In a matter of seconds, the first of these glistening creatures was on its way to Czechoslovakia. A man lifted it off the nozzle, walked to the door, and let it go, just like that. A circulation manager's dream. The station launched up to seven hundred an hour, each balloon carrying 108 newspapers, weighing one and a half pounds. I took a couple of balloons into the yard and let them go, watching jealously in case anyone else's should bump into them and cause the cargo to spill. In three or four hours the balloons would have landed and the following morning, a Sunday, the Czechs would be picking them up. Having seen the meticulous preparation and hard work, apart from the considerable cost in providing a simple thing like a non-communist newspaper, the Iron Curtain became very real, very close, and very stifling. It seemed rather appropriate that the balloons should be sailing into the darkness.

Over its period of operation, FEP sent tens of millions of leaflets, newspapers, and other written material to the countries of Eastern Europe.

The Manchester United Air Crash

A totally unrelated but horrendous event occurred on the afternoon of February 6, 1958, when a plane carrying the famous Manchester United soccer team crashed on takeoff during a snowstorm at Munich airport, killing twenty-three of the forty-four people on board, including eight of the team's top players and eight sports writers traveling with the team. The team's sainted manager, Matt Busby, was very seriously injured. There were no British reporters based in Munich at the time, so the few of us working at RFE jumped into action as stringers for the London and Manchester papers, dividing up our duties between the airport and the hospital where the injured had been taken, combining our information, and calling in updates to the British media every few minutes as the night wore on.

It was the most important story in Britain, Germany, and the rest of Europe for days on end. There were countless acts of heroism to report as individual players and crew sought to rescue passengers from the flames that engulfed the stricken plane, and as rumors began to swirl in Britain over the future of its most successful soccer team: would Manchester United survive? Matt Busby, hospitalized for more than two months and so sick that he was twice read his last rites, nevertheless gave interview after interview from his hospital bed to reassure the British public that he would be back and that Manchester United would regain its preeminent position in the annals of British and European soccer. At that time, few believed it would be possible.

Ironically, covering this story was the first time my byline appeared on the lead story of the *Telegraph*'s front page—though I had actually left the paper two years earlier. In the highly competitive rough-and-tumble of Britain's newspaper world, it was considered a considerable coup for the *Telegraph* to show that it had its own correspondent, John Adams, reporting on the scene from Munich, while other London-based reporters were unable to reach Munich for another twenty-four hours because of bad weather. These were the days before television news.

I would be remiss not to mention that Germany shared in Britain's tragedy. Several German civilians were killed and injured as the plane skidded off the runway and crashed in flames across a nearby road and into a family home, which burst into flames. Today, memorials commemorating the tragic events of that night can be found both at the team's stadium in Manchester and near the old airport in Munich. In 2008, the Munich city council named the site of one of the memorials Manchesterplatz (Manchester Place.)

Adenauer and America

Entente Cordiale

What can one say about Bonn? It was and remains a sleepy little town along the Rhine, whose chief claim to fame was that it was the birthplace of Ludwig van Beethoven, whose boyhood home had been turned into a small museum along a narrow side street in the old town. I lived nearby and visited it often, especially when I had guests. I have been a Beethoven enthusiast ever since. As a writer, I was particularly impressed by the number of times he vigorously scratched out and rewrote his music before being satisfied with it.

When, after the war, Bonn became the seat of the West German government, it was suddenly inundated with correspondents from all over the world. I felt very much at home. The head of government was eighty-year-old Konrad Adenauer, former mayor of Cologne and prisoner of the Nazis, who was perfect for the position of chancellor. His stamina was incredible. Aside from his political sensitivity in balancing the needs of his people with those of the Americans and other allies, he had a wonderful sense of humor and often had press conferences convulsed in gales of laughter. He would patiently stand for an hour or more taking questions from reporters, mixing serious answers with apt witticisms. He was much loved and respected by the German people, who felt he represented their interests well, and by the Allies, who found him eminently wise and knowledgeable. As a hobby, Adenauer cultivated roses at his modest home overlooking the Rhine. He recommended that all politicians cultivate roses because, he explained, it teaches patience, "the most important thing in politics."

The German government did an excellent job of briefing reporters. It was while covering news conferences in German that I discovered that Pitman's shorthand works equally well in German or English, since it is all based on phonetics. At that time, foreign correspondents' bureaus consisted of prefabricated huts known as the PresseHuette, erected like a little town on land next to the German Parliament building. Some complained about the heat or the cold or the mud, but I loved it. I got to know my neighbors at *The Economist* (a great source of information) and Reuters, as well as Georg Schroeder, the top political correspondent of the leading German daily, *Die Welt*, whose attractive daughter Monica came to work for me. All in all, we reporters were a happy family, well looked after by German officials and with not too many crises to worry about.

Even the traumatic construction of the Berlin Wall did not affect us too much—that was for the Berlin-based correspondents. Lyndon Johnson, then vice president, came to Bonn to meet and reassure the leaders of the West German government, whose mandate did not extend to Berlin, that they still had America's full support. At the entrance to the Villa Hammerschmidt, residence of the German president, Johnson stopped his car—a convertible—stood up, and started handing out ballpoint pens with his name on them to the crowds who had gathered. I was among them and was also among those who found this gesture quite ludicrous: demeaning for the vice president of the United States to be handing out ballpoint pens, and somewhat insulting to the Germans who had gathered around his car. They did not want ballpoint pens. They wanted reassurance that their country was not going to be invaded or abandoned. It was quite a long time before I realized that LBJ's simple gesture with the ballpoint pens was in fact a kind of reassurance in a "Don't worry, be happy" kind of way.

The huge American embassy in Bad Godesberg, just outside Bonn, was the mother ship for American correspondents—a great source of information from experienced public affairs officers whom you could call at any time, day or night, to confirm or discount rumors. They were always courteous and seemed to have background papers on everything of importance. For special visitors, they would invite a select group of reporters to the ambassador's residence for an informal briefing. This was how I met Ed Murrow, the famed wartime CBS correspondent who had retired somewhat unwillingly and was now head of the United States Information Agency. He did not seem comfortable in his new role and clearly did not enjoy answering questions from reporters. I ventured a question about RFE, which was obviously among those he did not welcome. He gave me a skillful non-answer. On another occasion the ambassador's guest was Averell Harriman, then an ambassador-at-large for President Kennedy. Harriman started quizzing the correspondents about whom we thought would win the upcoming German election, phrasing his question in the imperious manner then common among well-to-do Americans: "This is what we are hearing: what do you boys think?"

Sidney Gruson, the eminent *New York Times* correspondent, took rightful umbrage at being referred to as a boy, and explained very firmly to Harriman that we were there to ask him questions, not the other way about. Harriman quietly backed down. In fact, the U.S. government was hoping and expecting Adenauer to win handily, which he did. This is what Harriman had heard. But Gruson did not feel it was our job to act as research assistants to help confirm rumors. I thought he was unnecessarily rude to a respected American statesman, but I also admired the fact that

American correspondents did not feel as subservient as European correspondents typically did in dealing with government officials and politicians, however exalted their status. Gruson was the dean of American correspondents in the German capital. Another news veteran who considered himself at least as important was the legendary Daniel Schorr, then the correspondent for CBS News, who continued to be a working journalist—doing insightful radio commentaries for National Public Radio—until his death in 2010 at the age of ninety-three.

One of the nicest correspondents in Bonn was George Vine of Britain's *News Chronicle.* One morning he organized an informal breakfast for British correspondents with Felix von Eckhardt, the chief spokesman for the German government. Unfortunately, George heard shortly before this event took place that his paper, never financially strong, had finally gone out of business. As we went around the table introducing ourselves, when it came to George, he simply said, "Meine Zeiting ist kaput!" (My newspaper is dead.) We all felt for him.

Congenial as Bonn was, it was always a pleasure to get away. Part of my responsibility was to interview American and British correspondents on their way back from assignments in Eastern Europe, primarily Poland. I would usually travel to West Berlin to "debrief" the correspondents individually over dinner at the historic Kempinski Hotel. I loved the name and the James Bond atmosphere of the hotel and always wondered how many of my fellow diners were in fact spies. West Berlin at that time was full of spies, and I was always very careful about the table where we sat, and who the neighboring diners were, in case any of them could overhear us or might follow us out.

Hamburg was another of my beats while I was based in Bonn. We had a small office there, whose chief purpose was to keep an eye on shipping manifests of cargo ships passing through the port from communist countries, and to provide help to any Polish escapees.

One of the great pleasures of my visits to Hamburg was my favorite hotel, the Vier Jahreszeiten (Four Seasons). I used to write my stories in longhand while having dinner in the restaurant, and then hand them in to the hotel's twenty-four-hour telex operator for transmission to Munich. I would then pick up my copy of that day's *Daily Telegraph* from the hotel gift shop—and so to bed. Nearly all German restaurants had individual lamps on their tables, making it very comfortable to read and write before, between, or after courses, and this became a lifelong habit.

America's Catholic Press

Holier than Thou

The Catholic press in the United States is a formidable branch of journalism that is little understood outside Catholic circles. Virtually every one of the Church's nearly two hundred dioceses has its own weekly paper, most of them of high professional quality, some edited by priests, others by laymen, but nearly all flourishing. My immediate superior at RFE, Bill Fanning, had come from this milieu. Eventually he returned to New York as editor of New York's Catholic weekly, the *Catholic News.* I too eventually left RFE. Though I had no other job lined up, I felt that seven years in Germany was enough and was vaguely hoping to become a correspondent or editor with the BBC foreign service. I was also finishing a book on the political attitudes of the postwar generation of German youth. But before I heard from the BBC, I received an unexpected letter from Bill Fanning asking if I'd be interested in coming to New York as his deputy editor. Though I had been working for Americans for the past several years and felt I knew a lot about the United States, I had never actually been there, so was delighted to accept

Fanning's invitation. A year in the United States, I felt, would not only help to round out my education, but would also add a spark to my resume—perhaps making me a more attractive candidate for the BBC, or even, at long last, the Paris bureau of the *Telegraph*. Rather than a year, however, I came to spend the rest of my life in America—not through any conscious decision to do so, but because I felt no compelling reason to leave. For journalists, America offered opportunities galore.

The *Catholic News* had been founded in 1886 by Herman Ridder, an enterprising German American who had, a few years earlier, founded the ethnic *Katholisches Volksblatt*. The *News* started out as a national publication, but eventually became simply the paper of the archdiocese of New York—still an important voice for the Catholic hierarchy. The Ridders (as in Knight-Ridder) have been newspaper people for more than a century, beginning with a series of German-language papers for the swelling tide of German immigrants. When I arrived, the New York branch of the family was well established, and other branches owned successful newspapers and broadcasting properties in the West and Midwest. The current president of the Catholic News Publishing Company was Victor L. Ridder, Jr., grandson of Herman. He and his wife were part of the city's establishment and could not have been more gracious. But their paper, it seemed to me, was dying. Its design and editorial content were lifeless. A very obvious part of the problem was that none of the staff had any editorial experience. The typeface and layout of the paper were Victorian. It was printed out of town at the *Bridgeport Post* plant in Connecticut, apparently to save money. Money, or the lack of it, was clearly another major part of the problem. The Ridders did not want to spend more than absolutely necessary. Every time I made changes in the makeup to give the paper a more contemporary look, the printing bills went up and I was politely admonished.

One day a story came in from the Religious News Service saying that Hungary's Cardinal Mindszenty was dying—a big story for

Catholics everywhere, since Mindszenty had been for years a courageous symbol of the Church's resistance to communism. After a notorious show trial in which he was falsely accused of treason, he had been beaten and imprisoned. During the Hungarian Revolution, he was freed by students who carried him out of prison on their shoulders amid much jubilation. After only a few days of freedom, however, the communists regained power and hunted him down again. He sought asylum in the American legation in Budapest, where he was protected by international law. He was still there seven years later when this report arrived of his imminent death. I felt instinctively that the report was false, almost certainly planted by the Hungarian communist government in order to diminish Mindszenty's standing with the Hungarian people and with the Vatican. They wanted Mindszenty out of the way and a more pliant bishop appointed in his place. The Religious News Service was considered a reliable source, and every Catholic paper in the United States carried this important story about the cardinal's terminal illness. Except the *Catholic News.*

Instead, I telephoned the U.S. legation in Budapest and talked with their public affairs officer. He confirmed that the cardinal was in excellent health. "I wish I was in such good shape," the American official said. The cardinal walked a considerable distance around the grounds every day, he told me, and ate well, read extensively, and attended to his religious duties with no letup. He received regular checkups, and there was no indication of any medical problem whatsoever. We ran this story as a banner above the masthead on the front page to make sure nobody missed it. The *Catholic News* was the only paper in the United States with the true story. It certainly raised its profile among the Catholic media across the country. Bill Fanning, the editor, who recognized the importance of the story, was delighted. People were beginning to talk about the "new" *Catholic News*. I even received job offers from other Catholic publications. I knew better than to expect a raise from the Ridders, but was hoping for some acknowledgment of what was, after all, a major journalistic coup for their paper.

The only acknowledgment came a few weeks later when I was called into the office of the vice president for finance. He showed me a bill from the telephone company for nine dollars for the call to Hungary. In the future, he said, I would need to get permission from management before making any long-distance calls. I bit my tongue. There was obviously no point in arguing.

Cabbing with the Archduke

One of my oddest experiences concerned Archduke Otto von Habsburg, the oldest son and heir of the last emperor of the historic Austro-Hungarian Empire, who was a boy when the empire was dismantled and Austria became a republic after World War I. By the time we met, Otto had become an internationally recognized writer and lecturer on world affairs, warning particularly about the creeping encroachment of communism.

The circumstances of our meeting—at a communion breakfast at a parish hall in the Bronx—must have struck him as quite a comedown from the life he might have led as emperor, or that he did lead as the respected adviser to Allied leaders during World War II. I could not help feeling sorry for him. He was a fluent and knowledgeable speaker, with no trace of an accent, and the devout audience gave him a rousing ovation. Afterward, the organizers arranged for me to ride back to Manhattan in a cab with Otto and the other speaker at the event, the former world light heavyweight boxing champion Tommy Loughran. An odd couple, indeed. For most of the trip, Loughran was asking Otto questions about his life and I kept quiet. They were good questions, and Loughran was genuinely interested. But after we dropped him off at the New York Athletic Club, Otto turned his attention to me.

As the cab stopped outside the Algonquin Hotel, where he was staying, Otto told me about his syndicated column on communism, and how valuable he thought it would be for the *Catholic News* to subscribe to it. New York, of course, was an important audience for his views and possible future speaking invitations. Knowing as I did the *Catholic News*'s aversion to spending money on anything not absolutely necessary, it was with some trepidation that I waited for Otto to tell me how much his articles would cost. "Just four dollars a week," he said. He thought the price was very reasonable, and so did I. But I told him, quite truthfully, that I was not in a position to commit the paper to buying the columns. All I could do was recommend that they do so. He then offered to drop the price to two dollars a week. This had now become quite embarrassing, as I still could not commit the paper. But I did promise that I would do my best and get back to him. He was obviously disappointed. As I predicted, the paper was not interested. They didn't think their readers would care about Otto's views, or even know who he was. "You have to understand, John, this is not Europe," they explained unnecessarily as they pointed out that two dollars a week added up to more than a hundred dollars a year.

I wrote Otto a letter giving him the bad news. I did not hear back. But in the years since, I have often regretted that I did not offer to pay for the columns myself, out of my pocket. It could have established an ongoing relationship. I might have become his agent. Or we might together have turned his columns into an international news service. As it was, he did not need my help. He went on to become an influential member of the European Parliament and outspoken supporter of European integration. At his death in 2011 at age ninety-eight, he was praised by world leaders for his "strong stance against all forms of totalitarianism." I was grateful for the opportunity to have met him, however briefly, and still am amused at the thought of this kid from Hemel Hempstead haggling in the back of a cab with Archduke Otto von Habsburg, heir to the world's greatest and most historic throne, over a paltry two dollars.

Death of the President

President Kennedy, the first Catholic president in United States history, was assassinated on November 22, 1963. Day after day, it was the biggest story for every newspaper and radio and television outlet all over the world. We knew our readers would be expecting something very special for that week's issue. But what? Everything that could be said had been said. We decided to focus primarily on the front page. I worked with the printers in Bridgeport to reverse the whole page, so it was in mourning. In the center we showed a large profile of Kennedy, against the totally black background, but with no column lines and no text beyond the brief "Ask not" quote from his inaugural address in the upper right-hand corner, white on black. The effect was stunning. Everyone involved felt proud of their handiwork, no one more than the printers, most of whom were of Italian background, who put everything they knew into making sure the final product was as perfect as they could make it. Readers loved it. The paper was immediately sold out, and more print runs had to be ordered. Orders came in for months afterward. Often, my changes at the paper made the Ridders nervous. This time they were visibly delighted and gave me full credit.

Reporting from Africa

Around this time, independence movements in Africa were leading to attacks on missionaries, notably in the former Belgian Congo. Several priests and nuns had been killed. This was a very big story for the Catholic press, yet there were no Catholic media representatives there from the United States. I suggested to the Ridders that they send me. I could do stories that the paper could then syndicate to all the other Catholic papers, enhancing its reputation as the leading Catholic paper in the country. I was disappointed but not altogether surprised when they said no—on the very practical grounds that their job was to serve the archdiocese of New York, not the rest of the country. However, I did manage to convince Fanning that it would be a good thing to do, if we could find a way of financing it. An early supporter was the editor of the Catholic weekly in Camden, New Jersey, a big paper that served six dioceses. The editor was a priest with a genuine interest in the world outside Camden. Fanning found others, including the National Catholic News Service, where he had formerly worked. A friend of mine at a public relations firm also came up with some funds and an airplane ticket. Before leaving, I touched base with ABC News, where I had a contact. The news manager provided me with a tape recorder, and I became an official stringer for the radio network, which also, as it happened, had no one reporting for them from Africa.

And so I found myself reporting from as many countries as I could afford to visit, sending stories by mail to Fanning for further distribution, and doing recordings for ABC. My destinations included the French and Belgian Congo, Ghana, Nigeria, Angola, South Africa, Mozambique, Rhodesia (as it then was), and Tanzania. The stories—including interviews with a number of African bishops who were not used to being interviewed by American or European media (if you were white, you were usually considered European)—were well received by the Catholic media. Fanning was ecstatic. In the Congo, I sought an interview with the recently appointed prime minister, Cyrille Adoula, a Catholic, but could not get past his American public relations man, who invited me to his incongruously plush apartment for a gin-and-tonic on the balcony while he checked out my credentials. He told me to write out my questions and he would submit them to Adoula for me. Two days later, he invited me back to his apartment to pick up the answers. The answers were fine—just what I needed—but I couldn't help feeling they were actually composed by the PR man, one of my first uneasy exposures to that profession.

By sheer happenstance I was in Dar es Salaam, the capital of Tanganyika, the day that country announced its merger with Zanzibar and became Tanzania. This was a dramatic political event and the only really hard news I had to report to ABC during my trip. I went on the air from the studios of the U.S. Information Agency, in a forested area just outside the capital. The ABC producers in New York told me to begin my report by saying "Hello Flair." Because of bad connections, I found myself saying "Hello Flair" several times before I could actually begin. I felt silly repeating "Hello Flair" in the middle of the jungle, but in the end it was worth it. *Flair* was an upscale interactive program in which I was interviewed by the host about the prospects for this new African alliance, about which, of course, I knew very little. But I was the only reporter from any network actually on the scene, so my words carried weight— geographically, if nothing else. I reported that the union of Zanzibar and Tanganyika was not necessarily good news for the United States or the West, since Tanganyika's self-appointed president, Julius Nyerere, who had been generously funded by the West, was already an authoritarian figure encouraging a greater Chinese presence in Africa, and Babu, the Marxist dictator of Zanzibar, would only encourage this leftward drift. It was not until later that I learned that the CIA had engineered the union of the two countries to prevent Zanzibar from becoming an African Cuba. As it turned out, Nyerere and Babu did not get along, but the union held fast. Both the Tanzanian mainland and the islands of Zanzibar just off the coast remain major tourist attractions for adventuresome Westerners.

Angola at the time was a Portuguese colony and not overly friendly to Western media. Through my connection with the New York public relations firm that represented the Overseas Companies of Portugal, however, I was able to get in. I interviewed the American diplomatic representatives based there, housed in a small office at the top of a hill overlooking the capital of Luanda. They seemed surprised to see me, and they were so open in their comments— doubting that Portugal would be able to hang on to its African colonies—that I felt they also doubted that my report would ever get on the air. Censorship was strict, and I wasn't too sure about even getting my report to New York until I came across a priest who was about to fly to the United States and promised to deliver the tape to ABC News for me. Confirmation that he was as good as his word came in a telegram from ABC a few days later saying they had used the report. There are few more welcome communications for a reporter in the field.

Ghana was a joy. It was by far the best organized of the countries I visited. Its people, too, were joyful and proud in their newfound independence. And they couldn't have been nicer. Nigeria was messier. "The trouble with our country," a Nigerian bishop told me, "is that everyone wants to be a politician, make money from bribes, and own a Mercedes. Nobody wants to be a schoolteacher or engineer. Yet we need teachers and engineers. We don't need more politicians." Rhodesia, as it then was, was just like England, but with a better climate.

I loved Africa—its energy, its beauty, its exhilarating climate—and its comparative innocence. Africans had very few material possessions, but they seemed far happier than most Westerners. They were not spoiled. They seemed grateful for each new day. I would never forget the barefooted night clerk at the Hotel du Foret in Congo-Brazzaville asking with genuine concern who would look after Jacqueline Kennedy now that she no longer had a husband to provide for her. Nor would I forget the hotel in Johannesburg where I had arranged to meet a leading African reporter in the lobby, only to discover that he was not allowed in the lobby because he was black. There was so much to report, including the increasingly worrisome incursions being made by Communist China in Tanzania—incursions that have only increased in the years since, but are seldom if ever reported in the mainstream media. I would have loved to stay longer, but after two months I was out of money and had to come home. After a few weeks back at the *Catholic News,* my reports from Africa led to ABC offering me a full-time job as a writer in their television news division at more than twice the salary, and I soon found myself flying to the 1964 Republican convention in San Francisco. For me, a new era had begun.

ABC and CBS News

Goldwater and Cronkite

There was an aura about television. If you were in television, you were thought of as special, seen by the public as somehow superior to the traditional "ink-stained wretches" who worked for newspapers or wire services. Even waiters would look at you differently and ask for your autograph. This was heady stuff. You represented glamor. For those of us from a print background, it was an uncomfortable feeling—too close to the world of entertainment.

Even experienced radio reporters sometimes had difficulty making the transition to television. Dan Schorr was a good example. He had always been a radio correspondent and in the view of CBS management, did not understand the different needs of television. He also was not a pretty face, one of the new criteria for television success. They brought him home from Germany and planned to dismiss him, regardless of his many years of excellent radio reporting. His reports from Germany were no longer considered interesting enough for an American public now hooked on TV. Plus he did not have an easy personality and did not have many friends in the upper reaches of the news organization. But on arriving in New York, he fell sick, and while in hospital watched American television extensively for the first time. He wrote a memo to management saying that he noticed that the network news shows all tended to focus on the same issues—politics and foreign affairs—but no one was covering domestic matters such as housing, health, and welfare, which were potentially of much greater interest to ordinary viewers. After leaving the hospital, he was reassigned to Washington to cover health and welfare issues, obtaining numerous scoops. He proved himself to be a great television reporter—and became one of the first influential critics of the American health system, which he wrote about in his book *Don't Get Sick in America*.

At ABC News, I was assigned to the emerging documentary unit called ABC Scope as a writer and associate producer. The first documentary I worked on was on a subject I knew absolutely nothing about—a proposed amendment to the Constitution on presidential disability, to prevent a repeat of the situation when President Woodrow Wilson suffered a stroke and his wife, Edith, essentially took over his presidential duties and kept the public in the dark about his health until after his death in 1924. A colleague and I consulted numerous experts and labored over the script, which was to be read by Howard K. Smith, one of the most gifted writers and broadcasters in the business. We offered our script with some misgivings. The subject was heavy and our script was even heavier, too full of terminology and facts in which the public would have little interest. Smith took his pencil to it and changed the fact-filled first paragraph to read, "Justice Felix Frankfurter used to say that God looks after drunks, little children, and the United States of America."

How could anyone not continue to listen? The amendment on presidential disability and succession was finally ratified in 1967.

After working on a few more documentaries, on subjects as varied as Vatican Council II and the British general election, I was selected to join the ABC team covering the 1964 Republican convention in San Francisco—my first trip to the West Coast. The convention itself was held in a mammoth building with the unlikely name of the Cow Palace. I did not know what to expect—but was not disappointed. It was a historic event and an amazing experience. It was the convention at which Senator Barry Goldwater, "Mr. Conservative," was elected his party's nominee for the upcoming presidential election. The Cow Palace was full of his conservative supporters. The atmosphere was electric. When former President Eisenhower made some critical remarks from the podium about media bias, the phalanx of reporters covering the convention walked out en masse. When it was the turn of Goldwater's principal opponent, the liberal Republican Nelson Rockefeller, to address the convention, the delegates booed him loudly for more than ten minutes so that he could not even begin. When the booing eventually died down, Rockefeller's first words were, "Thank you. I believe this is still a free country." Whereupon the booing resumed for several more minutes.

Goldwater was nominated overwhelmingly by the delegates, and his acceptance speech was eagerly awaited. During the campaign, Democrats, liberal Republicans, and the media had repeatedly attacked him as a dangerous figure—an uncompromising extremist who would lead us to nuclear war. Some of his public comments encouraged this, including such offhand remarks about nuclear bombs as "Let's lob one into the men's room at the Kremlin." Though many of his comments were not intended to be taken seriously, they provided priceless campaign fodder for his opponents. His acceptance speech was bold, reflecting his conservative views, but not irrational. Rather than shrinking from those critics who accused him of extremism, he challenged them head-on by declaring that "I would remind you that extremism in the defense of liberty is no vice. And let me remind you also that moderation in the pursuit of justice is no virtue."

He never lived this down. I personally found it a quite acceptable position, in line with America's robust political traditions, but I found myself virtually alone in this view among the media, who went berserk, led by the anchormen in the television booths (Huntley and Brinkley for NBC, Howard K. Smith and Edward P. Morgan for ABC, and Walter Cronkite for CBS), who expressed shock and amazement that Goldwater would dare make such an "outrageous" statement, seemingly confirming all the country's worst fears. They were also clearly delighted that he had done so. This was the red meat they had come for.

"Grab It While It's There"

My own role at the convention was an essential but tedious one that most writers tried to avoid. I was assigned to monitor the hours and hours of video interviews made at different times of the day or night, noting the time and place and how far into the interviews any newsworthy comments were made, for potential later use. The best thing about this assignment was that it provided a lot of overtime, which the Writers Guild called "golden time," essentially doubling my normal pay. When I mentioned to my boss, a tough but kindly New Yorker named Tom Wolfe, that I may be breaking his budget, he put a friendly arm over my shoulder and said quietly, "John, grab it while it's there."

Goldwater was soundly defeated in the general election, but went on to serve three more terms in the Senate. He became a popular and well-respected figure among fellow senators of both parties ("to disagree," he often said, "one doesn't have to be disagreeable"). He died in 1998 at the age of eighty-nine, widely credited with fathering today's conservative movement and paving the way for the eventual political career of Ronald Reagan.

In contrast to the events at the Cow Palace, that year's Democratic convention in Atlantic City was relatively tame. President Lyndon Johnson had no opposition, though he tried to generate some faux drama by refusing to name his running mate until the last minute. Most observers agreed that this was unfair and unnecessarily disrespectful to Hubert Humphrey. The two men did not get along, but Humphrey remained totally loyal to LBJ, especially on Vietnam, at the cost of his own presidential prospects.

The most newsworthy event at the Democratic convention was the dumping of Walter Cronkite as the CBS anchorman, replacing him with Roger Mudd and Robert Trout, two seasoned reporters but "fresh faces" in the anchor booth. The reason was that, at the Republican convention, Cronkite had not succeeded in increasing CBS's audiences sufficiently, allowing Huntley and Brinkley to continue their reign as the most-watched news broadcast. (ABC, as anticipated, came in last.) Apart from anything else, the audience size impacted what the networks could charge for advertising, so this was a significant business decision. Cronkite, a proud man and eminently dedicated to his job as the network's anchor, responded to his demotion in a very gentlemanly way, though he must have been privately seething. In the end, Mudd and Trout also were unable to increase the CBS audience share and Cronkite was officially reinstated—reportedly at the urging of the network's owner, Bill Paley.

After the conventions, I was assigned to write for the ABC evening news programs. This was fun, in part because of the happy personality of the executive producer, Wally Pfister, a former writer for the Huntley-Brinkley show. The process of producing the fifteen-minute show was never the knuckle-biting procedure that I found later at CBS. The anchor for the show was at first Bob Young, a cutup personality from Terre Haute, Indiana, and then Peter Jennings, a serious young man from Canada who was very much a fish out of water. He was so inexperienced that no one could understand the move, until it was explained that Jennings's father was an important broadcaster in Canada and ABC management was anxious to please him. Jennings was eventually transferred to the ABC London bureau as a correspondent and years later returned as the mature and polished anchor of ABC's *World News Tonight*, which became the most successful of all the evening news shows. For several years, Tom Brokaw at NBC, Dan Rather at CBS, and

Jennings at ABC were considered the "big three" of television news. Jennings was at the peak of his very successful career when in April 2005 he announced on the air that he was suffering from lung cancer. Four months later he was dead, at sixty-seven.

In November 1964 ABC went through one of its periodic reorganizations and decided that now the elections were over, it did not need so many writers. Though I had not realized it at the time, my employment had been only for the election year. My boss, Tom Wolfe, could not have been more sympathetic. Like many executives in the business, he knew what it was like to be out of work. When he asked what I planned to do next, I told him I had no plans but might go to California to see if I could get a writing job in Hollywood. "Don't do that," he instantly replied. "You don't know Hollywood. They'll eat you alive." Better to stay in New York and keep in touch, he suggested. A couple of months later I was hired by CBS News. I had been recommended by a former ABC producer I had worked with, Paul Greenberg, who had decamped to CBS. He later became executive producer of the *NBC Nightly News* and a top executive at NBC. I have always felt grateful to him—though our relationship became strained when I declined to buy his British Triumph sports car. I knew too much about overheating British sports cars, and hardly needed one in Manhattan.

A few years later, after I had started a public relations firm in Washington, I received a call from Tom Wolfe, now retired and living with a new wife just outside Washington. During a congenial lunch discussing the good old days, he suddenly asked me, "John, what made you leave ABC? I could never understand that." I reminded him that the very simple reason I left was that he had fired me. After a few moments of silence, he conceded, "That was a mistake." I agreed. For the next several years until his untimely death from emphysema we remained good friends.

CBS had a stable of eight network news writers to cover all its regular news shows and specials, including those on the space program. With occasional illnesses and vacations, that meant that we usually had six who could be called upon at any one time. My first assignment was to write the midday and mid-afternoon news shows for Douglas Edwards. Edwards had been television's first anchor of a network evening news show, but had been recently displaced by Cronkite. I was then added to the team writing for the morning news, which was anchored at the time by Mike Wallace. Both were a pleasure to write for. Wallace in particular could make anything you wrote sound much more dramatic. Some days, I was scheduled for every news show—the morning, midday, mid-afternoon, and evening news, plus the weekend broadcasts with Charles Kuralt and Roger Mudd. Though it made for fourteen- or sixteen-hour days, it was great for overtime, and I soon learned that most of the writers had adjusted their lifestyles to a regular flow of overtime pay. I was also assigned to occasional specials, such as the Watts riots and the gold crisis. Then I was recruited to write segments for the space program, which Cronkite loved and in which I had no interest at all, but I couldn't decline the invitation. I was the assigned duty writer the night that Apollo 11 landed on the moon. I had little to do except stand by in case of a mishap. Luckily, everything went smoothly. As the world held its breath, Neil Armstrong stepped out of the lunar module onto the moon's surface and pronounced the famous words, "That's one small step for a man, one giant leap for mankind." I found this statement a little too contrived for my taste, but Cronkite was as happy as a sandboy. He had often indicated his desire to fly in space.

CBS was now in its heyday, with Cronkite easily topping the ratings. His success was well deserved, based on his unrivalled experience as a correspondent in and since World War II and his calm personality as anchor of the network's evening news. The latter quality served him particularly well in handling the assassination of President Kennedy in November 1963, when his soothing manner helped calm the country's very raw nerves. He became widely known as "Uncle Walter" and "the most trusted man in America."

Ending the Vietnam War

The Vietnam War dominated the news in the sixties, and for most of that time Cronkite reported the events dispassionately. This changed dramatically, however, after the Viet Cong's Tet offensive in January 1968, when the North Vietnamese army and Viet Cong launched simultaneous attacks on cities and towns across South Vietnam. This appeared to be a major defeat for South Vietnam and the United States, although the U.S. military and administration sought to present it as the opposite: a sign of desperation by the North Vietnamese because of the progress being made by the south. The American media on the ground in Vietnam clearly did not believe this version, and no one in the U.S. government or military seemed very sure what was going on. Was the Tet offensive a sign that we were winning or losing?

Cronkite, an old warhorse now in his fifties, decided to go to Vietnam to find out for himself. He was dismayed by what he found and aired his conclusions on February 27, 1968, in a commentary that led to President Johnson's announcement a few weeks later that he would not run for reelection. In journalistic circles it is often cited as a classic example of the effect that a single reporter can have on events. It is certainly doubtful that any other newsman could have had such an impact. Here is part of what Cronkite told American viewers that evening:

> It seems now more certain than ever that the bloody experience of Vietnam is to end in a stalemate. This summer's almost certain standoff will either end in real give-and-take negotiations or terrible escalation, and for every means we have to escalate, the enemy can match us—and that applies to invasion of the North, the use of nuclear weapons, or the mere commitment of one hundred, or two hundred, or three hundred thousand more American troops to

the battle. And with each escalation, the world comes closer to the brink of cosmic disaster.

To say that we are closer to victory today is to believe, in the face of the evidence, the optimists who have been wrong in the past. To suggest we are on the edge of defeat is to yield to unreasonable pessimism. To say that we are mired in stalemate seems the only realistic, yet unsatisfactory, conclusion. On the off chance that military and political analysts are right, in the next few months we must test the enemy's intentions, in case this is indeed his last big gasp before negotiations. But it is increasingly clear to this reporter that the only rational way out then will be to negotiate, not as victors, but as an honorable people who lived up to their pledge to defend democracy and did the best they could.

While everyone thought his position was articulated with grace and sensitivity, not everyone agreed with its sentiment. It was predictably popular with the growing antiwar movement, notably politicians and student leaders, but a number of Cronkite's colleagues were privately critical, questioning whether he really knew enough after a very brief visit to Vietnam, and whether it was our position as a news organization to be promoting a questionable government policy with very broad implications for the country. Some wondered whether he was simply parroting the views of one or more highly accessible politicians, such as Eugene McCarthy or Bobby Kennedy, who were carefully cultivating the media in preparation for running for president on an antiwar platform. The biggest impact of the broadcast was on President Johnson himself, who was alleged to have said, "If I've lost Cronkite, I've lost Middle America."

Preliminary peace negotiations began three months after the broadcast but moved extremely slowly. The North Vietnamese, feeling they were gaining the upper hand, were in no hurry. It was

January 1973—nearly five years later—before a peace treaty was finally signed, resulting in a Nobel Peace Prize for the chief U.S. negotiator, Henry Kissinger. But the fighting continued in various forms until the North Vietnamese army finally captured the South Vietnamese capital of Saigon in April 1975. More than fifty-eight thousand Americans had lost their lives in the conflict.

One night while writing for Cronkite, I wanted to check a fact and found the library was closed. It routinely closed half an hour before the evening news went on the air. That was the way it had always been, according to the chief librarian, and they weren't about to change. When I told the news editor that this was insanity, he agreed and told me to write a memo recommending what CBS should do. "A long memo," he added. So I did. The result was that I was appointed coordinator of broadcast research, with all the twenty or so current researchers reporting to me. No longer simply a writer, I was now an executive with a budget and a member of the CBS News management team. Part of my responsibility was to hire new researchers with the potential to become reporters or producers.

The first one that I hired, somewhat reluctantly as he was British and I didn't want people to think I was creating a British mafia, was a young Oxford grad and recent Vietnam vet named Howard Stringer. He went on to become not only an award-winning producer, but also the head of the news division and ultimately head of the CBS Corporation. By 2005, he was chairman and CEO of the Sony Corporation—the biggest personal success story in the history of CBS. Another hire was a young lady, Lorees Yerby, a California girl down on her luck and practically penniless, but with a great laugh. She was a creative writer, and I thought she had considerable potential. But before she could realize her potential at CBS, she left to marry the producer of *Hair* and travel the world with him and the show. I could always count on her for free tickets, she said cheerily as she bade me good-bye. Yet another hire was David Martin, the longtime CBS defense correspondent. In addition to new hires, there were a number of talented researchers already in place who were underused and frustrated. I tried to develop opportunities for them to become producers or correspondents, and several of them did so.

The top people at CBS News seemed pleased with the way the research unit was developing. They also expected me to know everything, which was both flattering and somewhat unnerving. A somber reminder of this came the night Bobby Kennedy was assassinated in the Ambassador Hotel in Los Angeles after winning the California presidential primary in 1968 and Frank Mankiewicz, his press secretary, was besieged by the media. It was past midnight on the East Coast when I received a call from CBS giving me this news and asking me to come in immediately. Bill Leonard, the vice president handling coverage of the event, had specifically asked for me, they said. I quickly dressed and hailed a cab to CBS News headquarters, just a few blocks away. As I entered the building, a guard told me to go to the newsroom right away. The night assignment editor in the newsroom told me to go right away to the control room in Studio 45, our biggest studio, as "Bill Leonard has been asking for you." I did not understand why, since I had no special relationship with Bobby Kennedy, but I was soon to find out. As I entered the crowded control room, a shout went up, "John Adams is here!" I felt I must be dreaming. Bill Leonard turned from the controls to face me and said, "John, thank God you are here. How do you spell Mankiewicz?" Bobby's press secretary was making important statements about the senator's condition but could not be identified in writing on the screen because nobody in the control room was quite sure how to spell his name (this was before the Internet).

Years later, I mentioned this incident to Mankiewicz over lunch at the press club, thinking he would laugh. Instead, he seemed offended that no one knew how to spell his name. (It was, after all, quite a famous name. His father, Herman Mankiewicz, wrote the screenplay for *Citizen Kane,* and his uncle, Joseph, directed such films as *Cleopatra*.) I took the opportunity to ask him whether Barack Obama, then running for president, reminded him of Bobby Kennedy. Not at all, he replied. Kennedy was much more of a leader. Obama reminded him more of Eugene McCarthy, the quixotic antiwar candidate Kennedy had defeated in the California primary.

Much as I enjoyed being part of the inner circle of the CBS news division, and the prestige that went with it, this was not really what I wanted. I needed to be closer to the action. I asked in vain to be sent to Saigon to head our news operations there, or to London to direct our European coverage, or even to head the foreign assignment desk in New York. But these were all coveted positions involving prickly personalities and internal politics, and I had never been good at that sort of thing. Around this time, I was offered a job in Washington to begin a congressional radio service for Congressional Quarterly. It sounded more interesting than what I was doing at CBS, so I took it—and lived to regret it. I should have curbed my impatience and stayed at CBS. After six months, CQ decided it did not want to start a broadcast service after all. But many more opportunities opened up at CBS. Should I go back and tell my former bosses that I had made a mistake? I decided not to. My pride, sad to say, got in the way of my career. But I felt at home in Washington, a very international city that felt quite European.

Public Relations and Public Affairs

A New World

My introduction to the world of public relations came in a phone call from one of the former editors of CQ asking if I'd be interested in a position in public relations. I was not sure what this entailed, but agreed to have lunch to discuss it further. The job, it turned out, was with the Investment Company Institute, the trade association of the mutual fund industry. I told him I did not think I'd be a very good candidate, as I knew nothing about public relations or mutual funds. He assured me that this didn't matter, as I could quickly learn what I needed to know. My experience in the media would be considered a strong enough qualification. So without further ado I agreed to become deputy director of public relations and advertising for the institute.

The offices were plush, the mahogany desks, full-length mahogany doors, and ultra-thick deep blue carpets bespeaking the industry's wealth and self-importance. When my boss first saw them, he told me, he thought he'd died and gone to heaven. It was extremely quiet. Unlike a newsroom, one almost never heard a phone ring or a voice raised. My job was also a quiet one—to write articles on such subjects as saving for retirement or saving for a child's college education. My boss, a gentlemanly former business magazine editor named Tait Trussell, was also very quiet. There was a lot of time for reading about various aspects of saving and investing. I became acquainted with such financial icons as Bernard Baruch and learned a lot about mutual funds and how they compared with other forms of saving or investing.

I also had the good fortune to become acquainted with one of the more recent icons—John C. (Jack) Bogle—who founded the revolutionary Vanguard Group of index funds. Bogle was chairman of the institute's board of directors at the time I was there, and very different from the other members of the board, who were all immensely wealthy and, in the manner of many wealthy people, had difficulty talking to people who were not in their business, or not in the same league financially. Trussell and I were not. We were just a couple of former journalists trying to do our best to explain mutual funds to the outside world. In the eyes of the board, we were "the help." But unlike the other board members, Bogle took time to visit with us and listen to our views, showed great interest in our work, and encouraged us to engage in new ventures—such as the launch of a new industry magazine, the *Mutual Funds Forum*, for which he wrote the cover story of the first issue, giving it immediate credibility in the industry.

More importantly, Bogle, who had studied mutual funds for his senior thesis at Princeton, was a severe critic of traditional mutual fund management. He felt it was far too generous to the managers, who quickly became millionaires, and distinctly unfair to small investors, who were burdened with numerous hidden costs they did not fully understand, but that ate away at the value of their investments: expenses such as commissions, advisory fees, sales loads, transaction costs, and excess taxes. He decided to do something about it. He launched a new kind of mutual fund known as an index fund, which would simply invest in the broad market (the S&P 500 Index) and rise and fall with the overall market, but would not be "managed" like traditional funds. As a result, management costs for investors in index funds would be close to zero, an immediate benefit for small investors.

Wall Street, which lived on commissions, was not enthusiastic. As Bogle has written, "The idea that passive equity management could outpace active management was derogated and ridiculed." His new fund, now called the Vanguard 500 Index Fund, was referred to as "Bogle's Folly." But Bogle persisted and received crucial early support from Nobel prize–winning economist Paul Samuelson. In a September 2011 article in *The Wall Street Journal*, Bogle noted that indexing has now come to dominate the field, with assets totaling $2 trillion, and that the assets of the Vanguard funds modeled on the S&P 500 Index, at over $200 billion, constitute the largest equity fund in the world.

Despite Bogle's enthusiasm and encouragement, it gradually became clear to me that the institute as a whole—largely governed by lawyers—did not place much value on the public relations function, at least not at that time. It came to do so later, as the markets changed and the institute acquired a dynamic new public relations director named Reg Green, a former top financial reporter who developed many successful campaigns for the industry. But during my time, the biggest challenge was to stay awake during the long, silent afternoons.

Relations or Affairs?

One branch of public relations is called public affairs. This means public relations involving government—or "public policy." Federal agencies are forbidden by law to conduct public relations, so they call it public affairs. The activities are the same. Thus the chief of public relations for the Department of Defense is called the assistant secretary of defense for public affairs, the equivalent, one told me proudly, of a two-star general. Certainly it sounds more authoritative than director of public relations. In reality, the Pentagon is probably the world's biggest public relations operation when measured by income and numbers of personnel engaged in press relations and other promotional activities. The White House, too, is a huge public relations operation, trying to convince the public by every known means that the administration—any administration—is doing the right thing, when there is often ample evidence that it is not doing so. Journalists are rightly skeptical of boastful claims and announcements by political appointees.

I gravitated into public affairs by accident. A friendly Georgetown neighbor named Jay Leanse, a Californian who had come to Washington with the Nixon administration, told me his agency was looking for someone to head up their public affairs operation and suggested I apply. I felt sure it would be a waste of everyone's time, but he was insistent, so I filled in some forms and did some interviews, which in my opinion did not go particularly well. These were not my kind of people, and I really wasn't interested. But to my surprise, I was offered the job and asked to start at once. This was somewhat intimidating, as I would be succeeding a man named Bill Helmantoler, recognized as one of the top public relations people in Washington, a former Pentagon public affairs chief who was most recently head of public relations for American Airlines. He was very well connected within the administration and particularly popular with the staff of the United States Price Commission, the agency in question. His job became open when he had to retire suddenly for health reasons.

My own public relations experience, by contrast, was minimal, and I had never worked for the government, so many of the standard public relations techniques and government rituals were quite new to me and I did not particularly like them or agree with them. I did, however, know the media, and felt I was a pretty good manager, so I agreed to take the job. I thought it would be a good learning experience, and so it proved to be. My rather grand title would be Director of the Office of Public Affairs in the Executive Office of the President. In reality, I would be the chief spokesman for

President Nixon's new and controversial price control program. Nobody could believe that a Republican president would impose price controls on the free enterprise American economy. Nixon did so in an effort to curb inflation, which was now up to 5 percent and seemed to be getting out of control.

Newsweek editor Osborn Elliott told us during an editorial meeting that he was driving home when he heard the news about the price control program on the car radio. "I was stunned," he said. "I had always hoped to be able to say 'stop the presses' and now, finally, I had a legitimate reason for doing so." The magazine had already closed for the week, but he immediately called his office and told them to hold up publication. He returned to his office to revamp the issue and particularly the front page to focus on price controls. An editor of the old school.

Wrestling with Inflation

Rumsfeld, Cheney, and Grayson

The Price Commission was part of the White House's so-called Economic Stabilization Program, headed by none other than a youthful former congressman named Don Rumsfeld, whose chief of staff was an even more youthful Dick Cheney. The chairman of the Price Commission and head of the price control program was Jack Grayson (C. Jackson Grayson, Jr.), the highly respected former dean of the business school at Southern Methodist University, who became my new boss. He was new to Washington, but had been strongly recommended for the price controller's job by then Treasury Secretary George Shultz, one of the wisest men in the Nixon cabinet, who had been impressed by Grayson when they worked together on a Ford Foundation project and especially liked the fact that Grayson did not carry any ideological baggage. Unlike so many other economists involved in public policy, Grayson would not use the price control program as a platform for advancing unrelated social or industrial policies. He was a problem solver, not an ideologue.

It proved to be a sound decision. In addition to his Harvard doctorate in business and experience as dean of two business schools, Grayson had a warm, accessible personality that appealed to everybody. He was also one of the most dynamic individuals I have ever known. He never seemed to sleep. Senior staff meetings were often well under way by 7:00 a.m., and action items for the day were on everyone's desk an hour or so later. Most days, too, meetings went well into the evening. Grayson challenged his staff not only to do everything that had to be done in a day, but also to go well beyond. He encouraged ideas and creativity of every kind. The place vibrated with energy. It was far from what I had expected the government to be like—and a very welcome contrast to my previous job in the private sector. He was also tough on his staff. On one occasion I thought I'd relax a bit by accompanying him on a speaking trip to Williamsburg, just a couple of hours away by car. There wouldn't be much for me to do there, and he knew it. So when I suggested it, he replied "Fine—if you think that's the best use of your time." Ouch! So I didn't go to Williamsburg, but I did steal the phrase for use on occasion in future discussions with clients and colleagues and found it to be equally effective.

While Grayson was a decisive leader and savvy about the nation's economy and price controls (he was essentially against them), he was not so familiar with the intrigues and machinations of Washington's entrenched political insiders. He was a registered independent in a fiercely Republican administration and suffered from the fact that he had no political base rooting for him. Critics could attack him or his policies with relative impunity—and did. This was his—and my—introduction to how Washington really works. No matter how smart or dedicated you are, you have to make sure you cover your bases. Grayson did not seem to appreciate that the highly partisan Rumsfeld would be a constant critic within the administration.

It also became clear that Rumsfeld did not appreciate Grayson's talent for publicity. He was a good speaker with a quick wit and received many invitations to speak to audiences around the country. When he did so, we would arrange for him to visit a local supermarket and patrol the aisles with a shopping cart, checking prices. This was a big hit with the media and helped to give the price control program credibility with consumers—as well as with retailers. The chairman of Safeway, whose office was in San Francisco, made a special point of visiting the Price Commission to tell us that if we ever had a problem with the pricing of any product in any Safeway store, anywhere in the country, we should call him personally and he would immediately get it fixed. He did not want to see Safeway's name in the papers for violating price controls. But Rumsfeld was not pleased. He complained that it was demeaning for a senior government official to be seen walking around with a shopping cart and ordered Grayson to stop. Most of us in the public affairs division thought this was a bad decision, driven by pettiness.

On another occasion, to reach leaders of the biggest corporations, we arranged for Grayson to write a major article on the price control program for *Fortune* magazine. It received a lot of attention, especially from Rumsfeld, whose PR man called me immediately the article appeared to demand that when any future opportunities like this arose, they should first be offered to Rumsfeld. What Rumsfeld's PR people did not seem to understand is that these opportunities did not simply appear out of thin air, but had to be created, and the Price Commission's public affairs staff worked very hard to generate them. Fortunately for us, the media were much more interested in hearing from Grayson, who was running the price control program, than listening to political spin from Rumsfeld.

Grayson was such a natural with the media that it was easy to arrange editorial board meetings with all the top publications, from *TIME* and *Newsweek* to *The New York Times, The Wall Street Journal, The Washington Post, Chicago Tribune, Los Angeles Times,* and many in between. For me, it was a great opportunity to get to know these editors and their business writers. As a former professor, Grayson was always very comfortable in front of an audience. At the Associated Press managing editors' annual conference in New York, he was slated to follow Ethel Merman—not an easy act to follow under any circumstances. After she had belted out "I Get a Kick out of You" to rousing applause, Grayson was introduced to talk about the sobering subject of price controls. He began with a big smile, turned toward Merman, and declared, "I get a kick out of you, too." It brought the house down.

One evening I accompanied Grayson to a dinner meeting in New York for selected clients of Bear Stearns, one of the world's largest and most aggressive investment bankers. It was a well-heeled, cigars and port kind of affair, and I was almost certainly the only non-millionaire in the room. Grayson was the featured dinner speaker. Shortly before he was due to speak, the host turned to me and in a whispered voice asked if I could suggest something cute he could say in introducing the speaker. I remembered Howard K. Smith's introduction to the documentary on presidential disability and said "Sure—try this." I wrote out on a napkin: *Justice Felix Frankfurter used to say that God looks after drunks, little children, and the United States of America.* (Pause for laughter) *We are lucky tonight to have with us ...* " He thanked me profusely, and I silently thanked Howard K. Smith.

Overall, I did not enjoy working for the government. I appreciated the opportunity of getting to know Jack Grayson—whom I considered quite brilliant—and top reporters like Robert Samuelson of *The Washington Post*, who went on to become one of the nation's most respected economics columnists; Brooks Jackson, then of the *Associated Press* and later with CNN; Al Hunt of *The Wall Street Journal*; and Phil Shabecoff, then a business reporter with *The New York Times* and later a top environmental reporter and author. I also became acquainted with Dan Seligman of *Fortune*, Osborn Elliott of *Newsweek*, and other top magazine editors.

It was fascinating to learn about the inner workings of

government—how decisions are made, and how they are sometimes mysteriously blocked. But the government itself was too much of a hothouse for my taste, with far too much internal politics and backbiting, where every word or statement seemed to be an opportunity for someone in the political arena to go off the deep end. Hillary Clinton famously called it the politics of personal destruction, and based on my own limited experience in government I would have to agree. I still have a memorandum from Don Rumsfeld to Jack Grayson complaining in haughty terms about a routine public relations initiative we were planning—and which he had heard about from someone, and wanted stopped, even though he was not sure what it was. His PR person could have talked with me about it and it would have been easily settled, but instead, Rumsfeld decided to make it an issue with Grayson. His curt memo read as follows:

> Two weeks ago I discussed with you the fact that the Price Commission, Office of Public Affairs (my department), was in the process of arranging a contract with North American Press [sic] Syndicate to develop some newspaper stories and cartoons and to reproduce and distribute the material, as well as collect clippings of the results. You and I agreed that this was probably not a good idea.
>
> However, I found out late last week that someone in your shop had gone ahead and prepared a contract to perform that work. Apparently you have not passed down your decision to not go ahead. If you have any questions give me a call.

Grayson was nonplussed. His cover note to me read as follows:

> Before I reply to Don Rumsfeld re the attached,

could you brief me as to what the content is. In a meeting with Don about three to four weeks ago he did mention that he had heard there were some cartoons being prepared and he questioned the wisdom of this. I agreed that cartoons might be in poor taste, but I didn't agree that we shouldn't have stories written to tell the story about inflation and the policies of the Price Commission. I need to know more about this before replying to Don.

The initiative we were planning was a quite routine one. It involved sending short stories on "mats" to small regional papers that would normally not have access to information about Washington policies and probably had never heard of the price control program. Not propaganda—just basic, very simple facts, normally with a cartoon-like illustration. It was one of the most widely used services in the whole field of public relations. Rumsfeld obviously was not familiar with it, nor did he need to be. Equally obviously, whoever drew this to his attention was seeking to undermine the Price Commission, or Grayson, or me. It was this kind of small-time mischief making that made working for the government so very unpleasant.

The White House eventually decided that its price control program had been a success—achieving the goal of reducing inflation to an acceptable 3 percent a year. To what extent our public outreach efforts had contributed to this success we had no idea, though we all received a small marble plaque with a message from Jack Grayson saying, "Thanks for making it happen." I received a second, somewhat larger plaque thanking me for my "profound devotion to the public service." The independent agency that we were all working for, the Price Commission, officially part of the Executive Office of the President, was disbanded. *The New York Times*, which had followed our activities closely from the beginning, carried a rare editorial eulogy, praising both our effectiveness and our fairness. Grayson and his senior staff certainly deserved it.

After praising the "firmness and fairness" of the Price Commission and its companion organization, the Pay Board, the *Times* declared, "They shattered the myth that controls could not work in a democracy in peacetime."

But now we were all out of a job (except for some employees on loan from other parts of the government). People wondered what Grayson would do next. Academia would almost certainly be too tame. He received several offers from corporations but turned them down. He knew what he wanted to do—and succeeded famously at his new career. He had concluded through his work with the commission that one of the root causes of inflation in the American economy was industry's declining productivity. As he looked into it, he was appalled to discover that neither the federal government nor most corporations had much idea of how to measure productivity—or how to improve it. Further, they did not consider it a serious factor in keeping costs down. The Labor Department, which released monthly productivity figures by industry, offered few guidelines; it just accepted whatever data companies submitted. And each company, it seemed, measured its productivity slightly differently. So Grayson decided to dedicate himself to improving the nation's productivity by establishing standards and educating and training business and government on the importance of productivity in curbing inflation and increasing U.S. competitiveness in the world. To do this, he created the American Productivity Center, now called the American Productivity and Quality Center, a pioneering nonprofit based in Houston but now famous throughout the world. It was the perfect match for his ambition, his energy, and his endless creativity—not to mention his fabulous skill at fund-raising.

As for me, for the second time in three years my job had simply disappeared and I had nothing else lined up. I later learned that this was not unusual in Washington, where political changes force people out of their jobs with some frequency. The smart ones usually see this coming and plan accordingly. I did not. Nor did I have many contacts among people who might have been able to offer me a job. But I was not sure I even wanted one. Though I had not been in the public relations or public affairs field for very long, and recognized that I still had a great deal to learn, I decided that this would be as good a time as any to see if I could make a living on my own. *I'll give it three months,* I thought. *If I don't have any clients at the end of that time—then I'll look for a job.* As it happened, I was able to sign my first client while still on leave from the government. Thus John Adams Associates was born—and went on to flourish for four decades.

*My cousin Patricia, who served in the Pacific during
World War 11, encouraged me to consider journalism as a career.*

*The author as apprentice reporter outside the offices
of the Gazette in Hemel Hempstead.*

Eaton Hall, country home of the Dukes of Westminster, on loan to the government for training infantry officers.

The author in Korea, overlooking the Samichon
valley near Panmunjom, December 1951.

The Radio Free Europe building in Munich in the 1950s. In 1995, the station moved to Prague at the invitation of Czech president Vaclav Havel.

The author at a memorial to Polish shipyard workers in Gdansk.

Poland's future president Lech Walesa shows appreciation for the media efforts of Ann Crampton in a photo taken at Walesa's request by interviewer Charlie Rose.

Conquering China. *Guided by Tom Buckmaster, a caravan of Airstream trailers made history in 1985 by touring rural China and making friends with local villagers and schoolchildren.*

Dynamic duo. *Former JAA intern Debbie DiMaio with her protégée, Oprah Winfrey. Debbie literally launched Oprah's career by persuading Chicago's ABC station, WLS-TV, to audition Oprah to host their morning show. She went on to become the most successful talk show host in the history of broadcasting while Debbie became the most successful talk-show producer.*

The author with noted political reporter John Fogarty, former president of the National Press Club and member of the Standing Committee of Correspondents of Congress

JAA's Michelle Kincaid with General Wesley Clark after organizing his TV appearance on White House Chronicle, the widely syndicated talk show hosted by Llewellyn King. The subject? Strengthening the nation's cyber defenses.

John Adams is 10 Years Old and Living in Washington

This year, John Adams Associates celebrates its 10th year of serving American corporations and industry associations in the nation's capital ... the third anniversary of its New York offices ... and its first year on Jack O'Dwyer's listings of the 50 largest public relations firms.

What kind of people are John Adams Associates?

They're the kind of people you feel comfortable talking with when you have a problem.

They understand public policy—how it is shaped and influenced. Many of their people have held key staff positions on Capitol Hill and at federal agencies. One of them recently took a sabbatical to run for Congress—and won.

10 years ago, they were helping clients prepare exemptions to price control regulations—and monitoring the actions of the Federal Trade Commission and other agencies for a leading Wall Street brokerage house.

9 years ago, they organized a huge gala at the Kennedy Center for Quaker Oats—and edited a book on energy policy for the Ford Foundation.

7 years ago, they began helping Jack Grayson spread the gospel of productivity from his Houston-based American Productivity Center.

5 years ago, they were at Dumbarton Oaks, organizing an international conference on the energy crisis with Saudi Arabia's Sheik Zaki Yamani and leaders of U.S. industry. That was also the year

they won a Silver Anvil for a national educational program on auto emission controls. And handled national publicity for MIT's landmark study on global energy prospects.

3 years ago, they received PRSA's Toth award for their annual fireworks safety program, headed up by George Plimpton. That year, too, they launched the North American marketing program for France's Antiope videotex systems and the new "smart card".

2 years ago, they helped the mutual fund industry defeat bankers' attempts to impose state-by-state bans on the sale of money market funds. And they expanded the chemical industry's nationwide media tour program.

Last year, they worked with former FCC chairman Charles Ferris to help the electronics industry fight off Hollywood's attempt to impose "copyright" taxes on all home video equipment.

They helped the nation's asbestos industry build support for legislation to solve the growing problem of asbestos lawsuits.

And they helped New York City get a fair hearing on Capitol Hill for its purchase of new subway cars at an advantageous interest rate.

Along the way, the people at John Adams Associates are proud to have contributed to better public understanding of such problems as dyslexia, juvenile diabetes, mental health—and the special plight of victims of street crime.

John Adams Associates Inc.
GOOD PEOPLE TO DO BUSINESS WITH

1825 K STREET NW, WASHINGTON, DC 20006 • 500 FIFTH AVENUE, NEW YORK, NY 10110
(202) 466-8320 (212) 921-1830

An ad in O'Dwyer's Directory celebrating the firm's tenth anniversary.

John Adams Associates

"We Need McDonald's"

I had never heard of such things as a business plan, and had no great ambition beyond making a living and providing a living for others when I could afford to. I wanted John Adams Associates to be friendly and informal with a minimum of bureaucracy, more of a news bureau than a PR firm—the sort of place where people would be happy to come to work, where the environment would enable people to do their best work, where they would be rewarded as well as possible, and where they need not fear losing their jobs if we lost a client. If necessary, as it sometimes was, we would simply take out a bank loan to tide us over. To the extent that this comprised a business plan, it was ours, and it was reasonably successful. We survived while numerous larger and more ambitious competitors fell by the wayside.

The most important reason we survived was the quality of our people. None had ever worked for a public relations firm before, but they had worked in the government and on political campaigns and understood how Washington worked. I was soon joined by three of my former colleagues at the Price Commission. The first of these, Dona Van Arsdale Jones, was an expert in government relations and seemed to have contacts everywhere, especially among Republicans. She handled our first Wall Street client, William D. Witter, a prominent research firm later absorbed by Banque Lambert. She proved to be a natural in anticipating their needs and providing prompt answers to their numerous queries about regulations that might affect their clients. She became a great favorite with the analysts at their New York headquarters. Her office was next to mine, and I can still hear her frequent peals of laughter and her favorite exclamation with emphasis on the first syllable, "You're *kidd*ing!" Esther Foer also joined us in those early days. She was a Democrat who had worked with Gary Hart on the McGovern presidential campaign and seemed to know everyone on that side of the aisle. So we were well covered on political issues. The important thing for a small firm like ours was to know whom to call for information in any particular situation—and we did. Word got around, and we were soon hired by a number of coalitions and trade associations on such issues as clean air, clean water, chemicals, electronics, fireworks—and compensation for victims of asbestos.

I should explain that Washington is a place where people come with their problems, where they want policies or regulations changed. It is not the exciting mecca of advertising, public relations, and marketing of consumer goods that one finds in New York, Chicago, or Los Angeles—or London or Paris. Hence, while often referred to generically as public relations, our activities are usually more correctly described as government relations, public affairs, or issues management—or simply, consulting. We eventually developed a particular expertise in scientific issues. Our chief scientist, John Heinze, with a background at the National Institutes of Health and in corporate research, was soon in great demand for his ability to quickly analyze new studies and determine how seriously they should be taken by our clients or legislators or the media. He was (and still is) frequently called upon to testify before government health authorities in Europe and Asia, as well as by such agencies as the Food and Drug Administration and the Environmental Protection Agency in the United States. His honest and straightforward approach also made him a major resource for the media, giving us a distinct edge over our competitors.

Over the years, our clients have ranged from major national and international corporations such as American Express, France's Aerospatiale, Canada's Bombardier, 3M, Corning Glass, Dow, DuPont, General Electric, and Sony, to such large industry associations as the American Petroleum Institute and American Chemistry Council, and coalitions such as the Clean Air Working Group, Environmental Industry Council, and Manufacturers of Emission Controls.

To increase our capabilities to serve some of these larger clients, we formed a partnership with similar independent consulting firms around the world and called it the Worldcom Group. I was its founding chairman and Andrew Edson, a financial relations expert in New York, became its honorary secretary. We worked well together and rapidly built the network to be the largest of its kind in the world, which it remains today, with more than 110 offices in fifty countries. Most of our partners are the best firms in their region, enabling us to compete successfully with the largest international conglomerates such as Burson-Marsteller and Hill & Knowlton.

In 1989, as communist rule was disintegrating, Worldcom became the first Western public relations operation in Eastern Europe when I established an office in Warsaw courtesy of my Polish contacts from RFE days. I met with Lech Walesa at his offices in Gdansk, near his old shipyard, and with other Solidarity and student leaders as they were coming to terms with taking over the government and civil institutions. I asked how we could help. Their biggest need, they explained, was money and financial expertise. "And we need McDonald's," they said.

"McDonald's?" I asked, thinking I may have misheard.

"Yes, McDonald's," they replied. "This is most important."

They explained that McDonald's was regarded throughout Eastern Europe as a symbol of American support and confidence in the future. It would boost the morale of the population and attract other Western investment. Without McDonald's, you didn't count.

Soon after, at a dinner in Washington, I had the opportunity of mentioning this request to the CEO of McDonald's, with whom we were cooperating on an unrelated environmental issue. "We are working on it," he told me, "but we haven't yet found the right soil in Poland to grow the special potatoes we need for our fries." McDonald's subsequently became a major investor in Polish agriculture, as well as an important symbol of American commitment throughout Eastern Europe. Today, it has more than 250 restaurants in Poland alone. And Poland, now a key member of both NATO and the European Union, is one of America's staunchest allies in Europe.

We were also asked to try to find an American shipyard to take over the run-down facility in Gdansk, which was totally broke and sorely in need of modernization. We made several attempts, not only in the United States but also throughout the world, contacting wealthy shipyards as far away as Hong Kong and Singapore, but none expressed any interest in buying or assisting the Gdansk facility. Its plight was too well known in the industry, which judged that the investment would have to be too great, for too little return. But we were later more successful in helping Jan Nowak (then retired and active in Washington on behalf of Poland and Solidarity) persuade the George H. W. Bush administration to make an immediate, much-needed loan of a billion dollars to the new democratic Polish government to help stabilize its currency.

Most of our work over the years has been related to public health, safety, energy, and environmental issues, and much of it—though important—has been more routine than challenging, often paralleling the work of Washington law firms. It usually involved helping our clients identify the problems they faced, and then developing appropriate strategies for managing or solving them. Methods employed for doing this—often referred to as tactics—typically include developing background papers, drafting congressional testimony, organizing meetings with congressional and regulatory officials, arranging media briefings, and writing articles or letters to the editor. Sometimes it may go farther, involving meetings at the White House and with key politicians and opinion leaders, or even a Capitol Hill demonstration.

Occasionally we have received requests from the White House. I happen to enjoy writing speeches and congressional testimony. I was therefore pleased but not altogether surprised when asked to write a speech for President Ford on the subject of inflation, of which I was now considered to be something of an expert, and later, a speech for President Reagan on the fiftieth anniversary of the Battle of Britain, with which I was more familiar than the regular White House speechwriters.

Occasionally, too, we have received welcome pats on the back from our clients. One, a former top executive of DuPont with whom we worked for several years, said in a note about our firm, "In my professional career, I have never worked with a finer, more competent organization. They set and meet the highest standards for their work and excel at rapid turnaround. They thrive in high-pressure situations."

An executive of another blue-chip corporation thanked us for our "candid and professional counsel." Many firms can write press releases, and design websites and content, he noted, but few provide the actual strategy to help with a client's business objective. "It is the strategy component that sets JAA apart from other firms I work with around the country."

Perhaps the compliment I cherish most came from a large trade association we have served for more than thirty years. In the middle of a conversation with one of their top officials about their latest crisis, he suddenly stopped me and said, "You know, John, we get proposals every week from firms that can do everything JAA can do—and more. They have more people and more services. Yet we stay with JAA. You know why? " After a short silence, during which I couldn't think of a reason to give him, he continued, "Because you tell us the truth. You tell us when we're being stupid. You don't just tell us what you think we want to hear."

I am glad to say we have also received occasional compliments from the media, the latest of which, from a respected Washington journalist, said simply, "I consider your approach to working with media one of the treasures in this town. Unfortunately, an endangered species."

What follows are some of the exceptions to our more routine work, often totally unexpected, which allowed us to work with such personalities as Congressman Charlie Wilson of *Charlie's War* fame, the irrepressible George Plimpton, and the distinguished documentary producer Charles Guggenheim, among others.

From King to Congress

This is the name of a historic and politically important documentary about the Reverend Andrew Young, the civil rights activist and former aide to Martin Luther King, Jr., who in 1972 became the first African American to be elected to Congress from Georgia since Reconstruction and later became U.S. ambassador to the United Nations. Our client, the Chicago-based Quaker Oats Company, had been concerned for some time that Chicago's large African American community did not participate actively in elections or in the political process, appearing resigned to their status as a permanent minority with little or no influence. Quaker's vice president for government relations, a public-spirited and imaginative civic leader named Tom Roeser, felt this attitude, though understandable (these were the early seventies), was bad for the African American community, bad for Chicago, and ultimately bad for the country. He wanted minorities to appreciate that they could not only participate in the political process, but by doing so, could also have a very positive impact on the way their country was governed. But how to get this message across?

One suggestion was to make a documentary—an exciting,

highly professional documentary film focused on Andrew Young's successful campaign for Congress from Georgia. It was a truly historic campaign—and conveyed exactly the right message: "Yes, we can." It could be shown in schools, movie houses, churches, and wherever else people gather. Roeser approached one of the nation's top documentary producers, Charles Guggenheim, who had won several Academy Awards for such documentaries as *Nine from Little Rock*, *A Time for Justice*, and *Robert Kennedy Remembered*. Guggenheim agreed to do it, which was not easy, as miles of film footage had already been shot and Guggenheim had to piece it all together, spot the gaps, and reshoot where necessary. He did a masterful job. Roeser knew that I and my colleague Clint McCarty had a background in television production and asked us to help Guggenheim as needed, since he had no staff. We were happy to do so. The documentary was completed in 1974 and can be viewed to this day at the Charles Guggenheim Center for the Documentary Film at Washington's National Archives. But it turned out that our work on *From King to Congress* was just beginning.

We were now given the assignment to organize a multiscreen premiere at the Kennedy Center, to which hundreds of Washington's political and social elite would be invited. The screenings would be followed by a gala reception and buffet dinner.

Organizing events of this size—we took over the whole of the Kennedy Center—was something new for us. Aside from the logistics of showing the documentary in four locations in the center simultaneously, the principal invitees had to be identified (everyone from the Speaker of the House and chief executive of Quaker Oats to Coretta Scott King and, of course, Andrew Young), invitations had to be sent, special seating had to be arranged, banks of flowers had to be ordered—and, of course, decisions on the food had to be made. These were just some of the myriad details. At one point Tom asked me to join him on the phone to help explain to Quaker's querulous executive vice president in Chicago why we needed to order three shrimp per head rather than just two. I couldn't believe we were having this conversation. But the whole event went off without a hitch, thanks to the organizational genius and delightful sense of humor of my principal partner, Dona Van Arsdale Jones. Everyone agreed that the Kennedy Center evening was a huge success, and *From King to Congress* entered the nation's political and educational lexicon.

It seemed to me that the subsequent election of Barack Obama from Chicago as the nation's first African American president was a fitting coda to the pioneering work of people like Tom Roeser, Charlie Guggenheim, and their associates, and to the generous commitment of the then family-owned company Quaker Oats, to the welfare of Chicago's minority community. Guggenheim, sadly, did not live to see Obama's election (he died in 2002), but Roeser continues his very active civic work in Chicago, where he is a popular talk show host, writer, and lecturer.

Lech Walesa and Solidarity

For several years, whenever one of the leaders of Poland's underground Solidarity movement managed to clandestinely visit the United States, we would receive a call from Jan Nowak asking us to try to arrange media interviews for them. We were happy to oblige. I usually passed the task on to Ann Crampton, our onetime intern who had evolved into our most effective media relations person. She was particularly adept at pronouncing their unpronounceable names and at explaining why every interview was important. In this manner, she came to know many of the members of Poland's future democratic government. Nothing fazed her as she repeatedly found herself having to cancel or juggle very tight schedules. The cofounder and leader of the Solidarity movement, of course, was Lech Walesa, the onetime electrician at the Gdansk shipyard and charismatic organizer of worker protests and strikes. He was awarded the Nobel Peace Prize in 1983, but refused to accept it in person for fear that Poland's communist government would not let him reenter the country. As his position appeared to become more secure, and that of the communist government less so, it was felt that it would be safe for him to pay his first visit to the United States. Thus it was that Ann and I were called to the White House to be briefed by Condoleezza Rice, then at the National Security Council, about the plans and expectations for Walesa's visit.

As well prepared as Ann was, handling the media relations for Walesa turned out to be a nightmare. Every major media outlet wanted a personal interview at specific times, and Walesa, essentially, could not have cared less. Ann had to deal with his Polish assistants, who did not seem to appreciate the importance of winning the support of the American media, and in any case were not willing to argue with their boss. If Walesa said he was too tired, which happened frequently, that was that. Ann was called several times a day by the same producers for the morning shows and the evening news, virtually insisting on an interview and incredulous that Ann could not arrange it. Walesa, it turned out, was more difficult to pin down than the president of the United States. Among the most insistent were the producers for Dan Rather, who could not believe that anyone would turn down the opportunity of being interviewed by the anchorman. "He has interviewed me before," Walesa said. "Why do we have to do it again? I have nothing new to say." His logic was sound. The only reason they wanted another interview, of course, was that it would be good for Dan's ratings, especially in important competitive markets like Chicago, with its huge Polish population.

One interviewer who refused to give up ("I'll go anywhere, anytime") was Charlie Rose. Ann eventually arranged for him to meet with Walesa at a wealthy Polish American home outside Philadelphia at 7 a.m. on a freezing cold morning. The interview went reasonably well, after which Rose handed Ann his camera and told her to take a picture of himself with Walesa. Ann happily obliged, but was surprised by what happened next. Walesa asked Ann to step forward and, knowing well what she had been through and sensing that Rose was being a little too self-important, he put his arms around her and told Rose to take a photo of them, which of course he did. This was essential Walesa, a warmhearted family man and workers' representative who despised pomp and self-importance in any form. A framed copy of the photo still hangs in Ann's office. The following year, Walesa became the first democratically elected president of Poland.

George Plimpton and Fireworks

In addition to his many attributes as amateur athlete, hilarious author, and editor of the literary *Paris Review*, George Plimpton was the country's leading fireworks buff and promoter. His book *Fireworks: A History and Celebration* (Doubleday, 1984), is the standard work on the subject. George came into our lives when my colleague Esther Foer and I called on him at his midtown apartment overlooking the East River in New York, to ask if he would be willing to work with us on a fireworks safety campaign. He greeted us in his stockinged feet, offered us coffee, and totally charmed us. Of course he would be willing to help. What did we want him to do? We wanted him to make a few television interviews and public service spots about fireworks safety on behalf of our client, the American Pyrotechnics Association, the industry trade association. It would be a pleasure, he assured us. So began a happy years-long association that contributed to the prevention of thousands of injuries, especially to children, and helped reduce overall accidents by more than 90 percent.

The fireworks industry itself was a client of John Adams Associates for more than twenty-five years. In addition to Plimpton's willingness to provide our campaign with high-profile credibility, there were other notable contributors to its success over the years, beginning with a mild-mannered chemistry professor named John Conkling at Washington College in Chestertown, Maryland, who also acted as executive director of the American Pyrotechnics Association. He was and is arguably the world's greatest expert on pyrotechnics and is recognized as such by safety officials of the federal government as well as by officials of mainland China, where many of the fireworks originate. The media loved him, referring to him as "Dr. Boom." Other major contributors to the program's success were the aforementioned Esther Foer, who knew everybody in Washington and was a great ambassador for the industry with government officials, and Ann Crampton, who acted as the chief spokesperson for fireworks safety longer than anybody, gave expert interviews, and was a great favorite with the media each year as July 4 approached. She even gave birth to her gifted daughter, Megan, on Independence Day.

Charlie Wilson and Chechnya

Before he became famous for his single-handed campaign to drive the Russians out of Afghanistan, documented by George Crile in the book *Charlie Wilson's War* and by Tom Hanks in the film of the same name, the late Texas Congressman Charlie Wilson also worked to end the brutal Russian occupation of the tiny republic of Chechnya in the Caucasus Mountains, a thousand miles south of Moscow. Chechnya had declared its independence following the breakup of the Soviet Union in 1991, and Russian president Boris Yeltsin signed a peace treaty with the independent democratic government of Chechnya in 1997. However, when the former KGB officer Vladimir Putin succeeded Yeltsin as Russia's president, he violated the peace treaty and invaded Chechnya with overwhelming force, conducting unspeakable acts of cruelty against the civilian population, including widespread rape, torture, kidnappings, and murder. There was no rule of law and is none to this day. In 2009, Freedom House declared Russian-controlled Chechnya one of the most repressive regimes in the world.

Enter Charlie Wilson. He turned up in our office one day, unannounced but unmistakable in his signature striped shirt and suspenders, and suggested we work together. He would handle Congress and the Chechens' democratic government in exile, if we would handle the media. We were delighted. From our office in the press building we launched a daily newsletter-cum-press release called "Chechnya Today" to keep the media and Congress informed, written by former Kiplinger's editor and press club president John Fogarty. We also wrote and placed op-eds and contacted numerous editors and columnists to generate their interest. My job was to coordinate with Wilson. I loved visiting his famously decorated congressional office, replete with weapons not only from the Afghan war but also from World War II, with an immaculately polished Spitfire propeller on the wall behind his desk.

Wilson was a great character and a true pleasure to work with. But he was also a realist. He knew that his health was failing. At a certain point, given the general lack of congressional or media support for the Chechen cause, he told me he might not be able to continue. He encouraged us to do so, but also cautioned that we were unlikely to ever receive any financial support. We gradually and very reluctantly wound down our efforts, while continuing to provide whatever support we could pro bono. It is unfortunate, to say the least, that the United States is likely to let its desire to "reset" its relations with Russia prevent any meaningful effort to help the Chechens. They have earned their independence. We can only hope that a new generation of courageous journalists, and other congressmen like Charlie Wilson, will not allow their cause to be forgotten.

Representing Georgia

Around 11:30 one morning I received a call from Enders Wimbush, a leading expert on Russia and the Caucasus, whom I had known for some years as the director of Radio Liberty. "John," he said, "don't go anywhere. The foreign minister of Georgia is on his way to your office." A few minutes later the foreign minister arrived, accompanied by a small entourage. They were looking for representation in Washington for the newly independent government of the Republic of Georgia, one of the first of the former Soviet republics to break free of Moscow's domination. Since it was lunchtime, I took them to Jean-Pierre, the upscale French restaurant next door to our office, and by the end of lunch we were the official representatives of Georgia in the United States.

For the next several weeks, we acted as Georgia's de facto embassy, receiving visitors and holding numerous meetings with the State Department, members of Congress, and Washington opinion leaders. At that time, the United States had no representation in Georgia, so we would get calls from the State Department asking all kinds of questions. One, I recall, asked if we could confirm whether Russia still had nuclear missiles stationed in Georgia. We called our chief contact in the Georgian government, an assistant to the foreign minister, who later called us back to say, "We don't know. You should ask the CIA. They would know best." We were also virtually the only source of information for the media. As Georgia's official representative, I found myself in the strange situation of being interviewed on television talk shows about any aspect that came to the producer's mind, from opportunities for trade and investment to where to buy Georgian wine and where the best beaches were. I found these interviews were pretty easy to do, since there was no one to contradict anything I said.

We greatly enjoyed our role as amateur diplomats, but unfortunately we were unable to achieve what Georgia wanted most—an invitation to the White House for Georgian president Zviad Gamsakhurdia, a longtime anti-Moscow activist. Such invitations to the White House had become a virtual rite of passage for the heads of newly independent governments everywhere, affirming their legitimacy. An invitation would have done much to consolidate the Georgian president's authority—and Georgia's independence. For whatever reason (and none was ever given), but most likely a fear of offending Moscow, the State Department would not agree to such an invitation. After years of living under the iron rule of the Soviet Union, Georgia found democracy difficult to handle and the internal situation remained volatile. Gamsakhurdia was eventually toppled by political opponents and replaced by former

Soviet foreign minister Eduard Shevardnadze, who, like Stalin, was an ethnic Georgian. The State Department was more comfortable with Shevardnadze, and we were called upon to handle the media for his first visit to Washington as Georgia's president. But he, too, was eventually ousted in Georgia's famous "rose revolution" of 2003. By this time, Georgia had established its own small embassy in Washington, a suite of offices above a Chinese restaurant on the corner of K Street. "Not ideal, but it's cheap," their ambassador explained with a wry smile.

Apart from anything else, we learned a lot about Georgia—its rich history and culture, its wonderfully hospitable people, its dramatic mountain ranges and beautiful beaches, its wonderful wines (we were paid in part with bottles of Georgian brandy), and its fierce sense of independence. Today, it is flourishing economically and is once again a major destination for Western tourists.

Afghanistan in Manhattan

One day I received a call from the National Security Council asking if we could arrange media interviews in New York for a number of Afghan delegates visiting the United Nations. Since we had an office in New York, it sounded easy enough, so I readily agreed. We were to coordinate with an American freelance journalist named Jere Van Dyk, who had just written a book on Afghanistan titled *In Afghanistan: An American Odyssey*, and who, we were told, would meet us at an apartment on Manhattan's east side, near the United Nations complex. It seemed an odd place to meet, but together with some of our New York staffers I went to the apartment and was greeted by Van Dyk, a pleasant young man who filled us in on the plan.

The Afghans, apparently, were here to win the support of the United Nations for ending the Russian military occupation of Afghanistan, which Russia had invaded in 1980. The apartment was totally devoid of furniture. So where are these Afghans? I asked. "Here," he responded, opening a door to what was presumably intended to be a bedroom. It was an amazing scene. Twenty or so heavily bearded Afghans in tribal regalia and headgear were sitting cross-legged on the floor, their backs against the wall. As we entered, they all looked at me. No one said a word. I asked Jere if any of them spoke English. "Some do," he replied. I greeted them as best I could, walking around the walls and bending over to shake their hands, saying "Hi" to each of them, but receiving no reply except an occasional grunt. They must have wondered who I was and what I was doing there—perhaps even suspecting that I might be from the Russian secret police.

Fortunately, Jere was in charge of arranging their meals and accommodations. All I had to do was try to arrange media interviews. My first thought was that our Afghan visitors would make a colorful picture story if shot in front of the United Nations. But photos, apparently, were *verboten* because of security concerns. It seemed that interviews with *The New York Times* and other major outlets had already been tried, without success. So with two of my colleagues—Joan Burke and Lori Rosen—we tried to convince every radio and television talk show within fifty miles of New York City that an interview with one or more of these Afghan tribesmen would be of great interest to their audiences. There were only two problems: most of them did not speak English, and those that did objected to doing interviews.

One who did speak English and who was available for interviews was one of the younger members of the group, on whom we came to rely for most of the outreach activity. He did not seem overly enthusiastic, and at times was quite surly, as if he were doing us an enormous favor, but we were happy to overlook his personality for the sake of getting the interviews. He was very good at detailing Russian offenses against the civilian Afghan population and against Afghan customs and tribal governments in general.

After the Russians left Afghanistan in early 1989, civil war broke out among the various Afghan factions and I was astonished to read that the leader of one of the most vicious rebel militias, who bombarded his own people and destroyed much of the capital, Kabul, was none other than the young man for whom we had handled those media interviews in New York. His name was Gulbuddin Hekmatyar. He had a varied career, fighting against Russians, Americans, fellow Afghans, and "foreigners" in general. He became a Muslim extremist and adventurer, who was twice briefly prime minister of Afghanistan, but essentially had no power base among his fellow Afghans, who distrusted him. Instead, he relied primarily on support from the Pakistan government and its notorious intelligence unit, the ISI, on the revolutionary leaders of Iran, on Saudi Arabia—and on the United States! Altogether, he seems to have done very well financially. According to some reports, he received at least $600 million in American aid alone. Today, wherever he is, he is recognized by the State Department as a "specially designated global terrorist" for participating in terrorist activities with Al Qaeda and the Taliban and is considered one of the three principal leaders of the Afghan insurgency. His targets have included President Karzai.

Jere Van Dyk went on to become a special correspondent of CBS News and a recognized expert on Afghanistan. At one point he was captured by the Taliban and imprisoned in a dank, windowless cell for forty-five days, an ordeal he describes in excruciating detail in his 2011 book *Captive: My Time as a Prisoner of the Taliban.*

Conquering China
in an Airstream Trailer

Perhaps the most remarkable assignment that ever came our way was accompanying a flotilla of Airstream trailers to China in the days when Chinese society was still very closed. They were not used to visitors of any kind from the United States and had never seen an RV before, let alone these shiny silver aluminum-clad homes on wheels, which must have seemed like visitors from outer space. The Airstream story is a fascinating one. Wally Byam, the company's founder, literally invented the RV industry, and the Wally Byam Caravan Club, an organization for Airstream owners who enjoy traveling in groups ("caravans") to different parts of the country and the world, became a social phenomenon. It was when they decided to make a first-ever trip to China that we were called in. The company realized that the club members would need help dealing with the Chinese authorities at every level, as well as dealing with an excitable Chinese population, who crowded around the trailers at every stop. The trailers and their towing vehicles, GMC Suburbans, arrived by boat from Baltimore and were unloaded at the port of Xiamen. From there, we took over for the next four weeks, managing virtually every aspect of the trip.

When I say "we," I mean one person—Tom Buckmaster—a hugely resourceful vice president of our firm with exceptional political and organizational skills. Though many years younger than the caravaners—mostly retired couples from the Midwest—he acted as a combination scoutmaster, tour guide, and general factotum, taking care of their every need with untold reserves of skill, courtesy, and patience. Following are his comments on what he described with typical understatement as "a formative experience."

Our assignment actually spanned three years, from 1983 to 1985, and included several distinct phases of work.

The first focused on creating the marketing infrastructure for the caravan, including partner recruitment, naming, branding, and trade media relations. Airstream saw this as an important strategic initiative, one designed to update their caravan tradition with a big dose of people-to-people positioning and global relevance. John and I sought to guide the client to a deeper appreciation for how this "event" could resonate with the general media and the broader public, becoming relevant—indeed inspirational—to those well beyond the travel trailer industry. Coming only a few short years after China's debilitating and destructive cultural revolution, Caravan America-China was a major investment for Airstream, a big risk for the Chinese, and an immense organizational challenge for John Adams Associates.

Each year the Wally Byam Caravan Club hosts an annual North American summer conclave, an event that attracts thousands of participants and their Airstream rigs, lined up with military precision by row and number, a shiny silver city emerging in a matter of a few days, turning a massive meadow into a unique zip code of rolling adventurers and storytellers.

Energizing this largely older, retired owners group was at the core of the second key part of our assignment, one that began with the logoed and flag-flying departure from the factory in Jackson Center, Ohio, bound for Lake Placid, New York, the site of the 1983 annual gathering. After a few days of tours, meetings, and speeches, the group headed south for a series of media events, photo ops, and overnights that took us by the Liberty Bell, the U.S. Capitol, and to a glorious send-off at Baltimore's Inner Harbor. There the trailers were hoisted aboard a Maersk freighter bound for the port of Xiamen in China. The American portion of the caravan afforded wonderful local and regional media opportunities and provided critical seasoning to the ten trailer families who comprised our first group. Their ages ranged from fifty to ninety and they were led by a dapper and proud Frank Sargent, a retired automotive engineer who, among other notable achievements, invented the Porta Potti®. These genial travelers were irresistible to print and broadcast media alike.

We knew this was a Norman Rockwell moment if we could let the authenticity and originality of the story shine through. And it did.

Many months later, in September 1985, the most memorable part of our Airstream project began. The caravaners met their rigs in Fujian Province and began their 1,500-mile journey through back roads and villages, highways, and cities of a China just waking from its cultural nightmare.

It's easy to recall the wide-eyed astonishment that characterized the puzzled greetings that met the group each time they stopped, and the crowds that multiplied wherever we paused for gas or sightseeing or to make a camp for the night. The journey was a challenging one; the roads were often unpaved or barely so and jammed with bicycles, not the cars and lorries of today's modern China. Just finding diesel fuel took untold extra hours, and fresh food was in short supply, at least in the quantities and types our Americans were used to finding with ease at home.

As tired as they were, I never heard a cross word or a complaint of any kind throughout this extraordinary adventure. These men and women were part of something important, and they knew it. Each time they tired or spirits flagged, a small village would welcome them and schools would empty their classrooms for an impromptu firsthand lesson in globalization. The caravaners' energy would instantly return, small gifts would be exchanged, and a cup of tea would cement another bit of friendship and understanding.

That trip, from Xiamen through Zhengzhou, Quanzhou, and Putian, on to Fuzhou, still resonates in my heart, informing the work I still do with a measure of humility and authenticity that great stories always have at their core. Formative indeed.

Tom went on to a distinguished career as the highly effective head of corporate communications for Honeywell International.

The Exxon Valdez

On the Rocks

When a supertanker named the *Exxon Valdez* quietly slipped out of the tiny Alaskan port of Valdez on a freezing night in March 1989, with a cargo of fifty-five million gallons of crude oil from Prudhoe Bay, nothing seemed amiss. The waters of Prince William Sound were calm, and the crew had navigated them many times. The captain, who'd had a few farewell drinks with friends at his favorite tavern before boarding the ship, handed over navigation to his competent third mate and went below for a nap.

He had just fallen asleep when the calm was suddenly shattered. The huge tanker, whose radar was not working properly, crashed into a hidden rock formation known as the Bligh Reef, tearing a huge hole in the hull and disgorging millions of gallons of oil into the pristine waters of the sound. It became the worst environmental disaster in U.S. history.

With a population of less than four thousand, Valdez is a pretty little town some three hundred miles southwest of Anchorage. As America's northernmost ice-free port, since 1977 it has been the terminus of the vast eight-hundred-mile Alyeska pipeline system, which has brought billions of gallons of crude oil from Prudhoe Bay on Alaska's North Slope to waiting tankers, enriching the state government and Alaska's citizens, who all receive a share of the pipeline's profits and pay no state taxes. One of the great engineering feats of the twentieth century, the pipeline was generally regarded as superbly designed, well constructed, and efficiently managed. It was owned by a consortium of oil companies, the majority shareholder of which was British Petroleum. It was such an important part of Alaska's economy that the managers of the pipeline were said to have begun thinking of themselves as the state's de facto government, often overshadowing the state's governor and legislature. This inevitably led to tensions, which exploded when news broke of the huge oil spill in one of the state's great fishery and wildlife centers.

There was plenty of blame to go around. First, everyone blamed the ship's captain, Joseph Hazelwood, for being asleep instead of at the ship's helm. Others blamed the third mate for not being sufficiently alert. Still others blamed the pipeline company, which had primary responsibility for responding to such emergencies but was extremely slow, due in part to heavy snow that had buried rescue launches and equipment. Then everyone blamed Exxon, which for the next several years was sued for billions of dollars for destruction of the local economy. The Democratic governor, Steve Cowper, had apparently taken it upon himself to place primary blame on the pipeline company—in part, it was said, as payback for the many slights he had suffered at the hands of the pipeline's managers, who provided the state government with nearly all its income and didn't let him forget it.

A week or two later, I received a call from our Worldcom partner in Alaska asking me to be part of an emergency crisis management team the pipeline company wanted to put together. And, of course, it had to be done right away. My first instinct was to decline. After looking at a map, I suggested taking part by phone, but that would not be good enough, they told me. I needed to be there in person.

I had never been to Alaska before, and as I looked out from the plane as we approached Anchorage I found the landscape almost unbelievable—endless snow-covered mountains as far as the eye could see. Very few townships of any size. No highways. But more small private planes parked at the airport than I had ever seen in my life. This was apparently the chief means of transportation. The climate was bracing, with sunny, cool days and very cold nights, but we did not spend a lot of time out of doors. We were whisked immediately to a hotel and spent most of our time there for the next several days, doing interviews and discussing strategy.

Our host, it turned out, was not the pipeline company, but a very pleasant and obviously capable public relations man from British Petroleum's American headquarters in Cleveland. He briefed us on the situation, including the tensions with the governor, arranged for us to interview key members of the pipeline company, and showed us copies of the local paper, which carried the governor's views and were therefore part of the "problem." Our role was to digest and discuss all the information and recommend a strategy. Since British Petroleum was the majority shareowner of the pipeline, the public relations man was essentially our client, though officially he was just helping us. The following day, he flew us in his BP corporate jet out over Prince William Sound to witness the extent of the oil spill, and then to the airstrip in Valdez (which had no road or rail link to Anchorage, which created a major logistical problem for rescue operations). He took us to several community centers, where volunteers were painstakingly trying to remove the oil from the wings of stricken birds, including more than two hundred bald eagles. It was fascinating to watch this world-class public relations man in action. He hugged the workers, who were mostly local women, grief-stricken by what had happened, and again and again asked them if they had everything they needed and told them to let him know if there was anything else they wanted. He would bring it to them without fail the following day. It was apparent that they were all very fond of him. As far as they were concerned, he and BP could do no wrong.

(Though Exxon was at the center of the crisis, the company sent no public relations staff to the scene until much later. Instead, they relied on statements issued from their corporate headquarters in New York City, where Exxon's CEO, Lawrence Rawl, downplayed the importance of the event and told the media he had no intention of visiting Alaska. He was pilloried in the press for his attitude and featured on the cover of *TIME* magazine as an example of an uncaring CEO out of touch with reality.)

It was a very different scene when, back at the hotel, we interviewed a senior executive of the pipeline management company, who exhibited what came across as a serious attitude problem. He obviously did not like being in the position of having to answer our questions, and it showed. He was very tense. His answers were curt. The company had done nothing wrong. The rescue operation in Prince William Sound had gone as well as could be expected. The state government was useless and had provided no help at all. The only light moment came when we asked him if the company had a crisis communications plan. Of course, he replied, adding that they had paid Hill & Knowlton, a major public relations firm, $20,000 to prepare it. It was this thick, he said, indicating that it was at least six inches deep. "Did you find it helpful?" I asked.

"No," he responded.

"Why not?"

"We couldn't find it."

"You couldn't find it?"

"That's right—and we didn't have time to look for it." There was a lesson here, I thought, for any company that pays $20,000 for a crisis communications plan.

After more interviews and a couple of days of discussions within our crisis team, we all agreed that our first recommendation would be a change of management at the top of the pipeline company. Relations with the governor's office had obviously deteriorated to the point where, in our view, they could not be restored. When we relayed this conclusion to the BP public relations man, he agreed, but helpfully suggested appropriate wording. It was clear it needed to be our recommendation, not his. It dawned on us that this was the real reason we had been invited to Alaska. BP already knew what it wanted to do, but needed an outside opinion. We offered several other recommendations for improving the pipeline company's relations with the state's legislators, as well as with the local and national media.

But our most unexpected recommendation, which took even our friendly host by surprise, was that the oil industry should invest in creating an international oil spill research center in Valdez, making the name of the town synonymous with solutions rather than with the disaster for which it was now notorious. In the end, the proposal was not taken up. The reasons we were given was that it would be too expensive, that the Exxon Valdez was a one-time event, and that the crisis would eventually pass. I think now as I thought then that the industry's decision was shortsighted.

Twenty years and many spills later, scientists were finding that the effects of the Valdez spill were far greater and longer-lasting than anyone anticipated, and that it would take many more years for some of the Arctic shoreline habitats to recover. Toxic oil from the spill continues to kill seabirds and marine life in and around Prince William Sound and many miles beyond. And after spending three billion dollars on cleanup, compensation, and legal expenses, Exxon still faces millions of dollars in claims—far more, in retrospect, than they would ever have had to spend on establishing a research center, an action that conceivably would have earned them and the whole industry some badly needed goodwill.

Footnote: Shortly before the *Exxon Valdez* accident, we had been awarded a million-dollar contract by the American Petroleum Institute to develop grassroots support for drilling in Alaska's Arctic National Wildlife Refuge. It was our first-ever million-dollar contract. Our proposal was so well researched and well presented that we beat out the nation's biggest national firms. Before we could celebrate, however, the *Exxon Valdez* hit the rock in Prince William Sound and our client sensibly concluded that "the time was no longer right" to campaign for drilling in the wildlife refuge. We didn't disagree. Our environmental friends were delighted.

Psychiatry Inc.

Having been blessed with reasonably good genes, I had never felt much need to worry about health problems or to take much interest in the intricacies of health care and its many related issues. My relatives were all fairly healthy and, as a reporter, I had never been assigned to the health beat. So it was rather ironic that my first client should be in the field of mental health, concerned with matters of hospital management and reimbursement for services. The client was a for-profit company known as the Psychiatric Institutes of America (PIA), whose business model was to create a chain of psychiatric hospitals that would be 50 percent owned by the parent company and 50 percent owned by local groups of psychiatrists. The doctors would bring in the patients, and the parent company would provide administration and management expertise. It was a profitable model, but the company had grown to the point where it felt it needed help with marketing and public relations. I had met one of their executives at a Christmas party, and he seemed to feel that our young firm was just what they were looking for.

My first task was to fly to Honolulu to manage an exhibit at the annual meeting of the American Psychiatric Association, where

I was to explain the benefits of the PIA model to anyone who stopped by the booth, and to get their names, addresses, and phone numbers for subsequent follow-up. In short, I had now become a salesman. The PIA booth was located next to the *Encyclopaedia Britannica*'s, so I got to chatting with its manager during the long lulls. Whenever a psychiatrist appeared, my neighbor would jump into action, shouting, "Hey, doc, got any kids?" It made me feel that I wasn't doing enough to attract attention to the PIA booth, except as a convenient refuge from the *Britannica*. If they didn't in fact have any kids, or didn't need more encyclopedias, perhaps I could sell them a mental hospital. The client eventually seemed satisfied enough with the thirty or so "prospects" I managed to sign up.

The PIA specialized in child and adolescent psychiatry. One of its showcases was the Elmcrest Psychiatric Institute, located in an upscale residential area of Middletown, Connecticut. I was invited to visit the facility to better understand how they handled their young patients. The medical director was a distinguished member of the faculty of the Yale medical school. We met in his office in a charming old converted mansion.

After a few minutes, the hospital's administrator burst into the office to announce that one of their female patients had climbed to the top of the giant conifer between the offices and the entrance to the complex, and was yelling obscenities at the top of her voice. She easily could be heard by people in the nearby homes in this otherwise quiet neighborhood. Other teenage patients had gathered at the foot of the tree and were cheering her on. "I'm going to call the fire department," the administrator announced.

"You can't do that; it will upset the neighborhood," said the medical director, whose name was Lou. "I'll go out and talk her into climbing down."

"It won't work."

"Yes it will, just watch."

We all trooped out to the tree, and Lou started calling up to the young patient, urging her to climb down—when she was ready—"so we can talk."

He offered to climb up to join her. This effort at persuasion was met by a new string of obscenities about Lou's girth and everything that was allegedly wrong with the hospital and her treatment. She was not coming down, period. Just as I was wondering how all this would play out, a siren could be heard and a huge fire truck drove through the institute's gates. The girl in the tree fell silent.

"Where is she?" demanded the fire chief.

"Up there," said the administrator, pointing.

"What's her name?"

"Wendy."

Before any of us could say anything further, the fire chief shouted through his bullhorn, "Wendy, I'm going to count to ten. If you are not down before I get to ten, I'm turning the hoses on you."

Without a word, Wendy climbed down and ran to her dorm.

"Is that all?" asked the fire chief. Lou and the administrator assured him that there was nothing further, and thanked him for his effort. I couldn't help feeling that the chief had taught them something valuable about teenage psychology, if not psychiatry.

Lou and I returned to his office and resumed our discussion about Elmcrest's innovative medical procedures. "Of course, it wasn't really necessary to call out the fire department; I could have talked her down," Lou assured me, sounding somewhat chastened.

"Sure," said the administrator as he took his leave.

The Psychiatric Institute of Washington also specialized in adolescent treatment programs. Its most famous patient, John Gilreath, was a repeat offender who had been referred to the institute by the court system, with the order that he not be released without the court's permission. After a year of treatment as a residential patient, his psychiatrist judged that he could be safely released into the community, requiring continued support only from an external therapy group. This turned out to be a fatal error of judgment by the psychiatrist and all others involved in the decision. They also neglected to inform the court.

Soon after his release, Gilreath, a strapping twenty-two-year-old nearly seven feet tall, waded across the Potomac River and climbed an embankment onto the grounds of an exclusive private girls' school, Madeira. There, in a secluded wooded area of the grounds, he came across a slightly built fourteen-year-old student named Tasha, the daughter of an American diplomat and Russian mother. She was walking back alone from the school chapel. Gilreath overpowered her, gagged her to stifle her screams, brutalized her physically, and tied her to a tree, where she eventually died of her wounds, shock, and exposure in the freezing air. More than twelve hours passed before her body was found. Gilreath was tried for murder and sentenced to fifty years in prison. He repeatedly applied for parole. I don't know how much of his sentence he eventually served, but it was assuredly not enough for a truly heinous crime that could so easily have been avoided. (The devastating and lasting effect of this tragedy was told in searing detail by the victim's sister, Helen, in the magazine *Marie Claire* of January 10, 2010.)

The media were all over the story, and all calls to PIA were referred to me. None of the psychiatrists or top management of the company would talk to the media. They couldn't do so for professional reasons, they explained, because of the confidentiality of the doctor-patient relationship. They wouldn't even talk to me about it, making it impossible for me to respond intelligently to media queries. I found this attitude quite incredible and questioned the validity of the doctor-patient relationship when the patient was known to be a brutal murderer. All to no avail. The doctors, business managers, and general counsel of PIA presumably feared lawsuits more than any breach of medical ethics. They also feared that business for the Psychiatric Institute of Washington would plummet after all the bad publicity. Ironically, and somewhat pathetically, this was not the case. Instead, business boomed as psychiatrists all over the country read about the case and called to refer their adolescent patients to the institute.

The PIA doctors and business managers were delighted. Their business model was working. The murder was already a thing of the past. They eventually sold the company for many millions of dollars.

Oprah Who?

Oprah would never have become so famous, so soon, if it hadn't been for one of our interns. Debbie DiMaio had just graduated from the University of Maryland when she joined us. A self-described "army brat" and totally fearless, she refused to be intimidated by self-important reporters or anyone else. She would never take "no" for an answer. I can still hear her telling one reporter over the phone, "C'mon, don't give me that guff—you know very well that this is a good story. Let's talk about it." She loved to banter with the media, and they seemed to appreciate it. They found her refreshing.

Debbie had a quick wit and a sparkling laugh, which made her fun to work with. Nothing got her down. But good as she was at our business, she made no secret of the fact that she really wanted to work in television. We did not discourage her, because we knew that television would be more fun and she would do well. It was a great world for young people with the necessary moxie. Though it was difficult to break in, we realized it would be only a matter of time before Debbie did so. Sooner than we expected, she informed us that she had landed a job as an associate producer with a little-known morning show in Baltimore. The show itself, she confided, was "beyond banal." The only bright spot was working with the show's anchor, a bright young African American woman from the Deep South named Oprah Winfrey.

As soon as she could, Debbie moved on to a better job as a producer with one of the nation's biggest regional stations, the ABC-owned-and-operated Channel 7 (WLS-TV) in Chicago. She was assigned to its then low-rated morning talk show, *AM Chicago*, whose longtime host had recently departed. The station was auditioning potential successors. Debbie urged the station's management to consider Oprah. They were not enthusiastic. "We don't think our audience is ready for a woman in that slot," they told her.

Debbie persisted. At least they should give Oprah an audition before making their decision, she argued. Reluctantly, they did so. They brought Oprah to Chicago for a tryout. Debbie organized a series of fake interviews so they could see Oprah in action, and in an aside to her old friend, she begged Oprah to be careful not to screw things up. The station manager, Dennis Swanson, who had only recently joined the station to rescue it from poor ratings, was enormously impressed. Oprah was an immediate hit. In less than a year, the morning show had shot to first place and was soon picked up nationally under its new name, *The Oprah Winfrey Show*. Channel 7, meanwhile, regained its lead as the highest-rated news station in Chicago. As everyone knows, Oprah went on to become the most successful TV personality the world has ever known.

For the next several years, Debbie was executive producer of the show and president of Oprah's independent multimedia production company, Harpo Productions. She selected the topics and personalities for Oprah to interview, and the show made headlines, often national headlines, day after day.

As its ratings soared, Debbie became one of the most successful television producers in the United States. But what we, her former colleagues, most appreciated was that she never lost touch. She would call periodically just to chat and laugh and see how we were doing. And she would always return our calls. She's a wonderfully warm human being with a huge heart, a great sense of humor—and a natural talent for knowing what Americans want to watch on television.

Breaking the Glass Ceiling

A Generation of Achievers

Oprah and Debbie are perhaps the two most obvious examples of how women in recent years have come to dominate the media. In many ways, they *are* the media. Barbara Walters, of course, was the first to break through the glass ceiling of network news. Her very readable memoir, *Audition,* tells of the quite astonishing amount of prejudice she had to overcome before being taken seriously. In a way, she paved the way for Oprah. But now, many of the chief executives of the nation's biggest and most successful companies are women. Women increasingly hold top posts in the federal government and in governors' mansions. So it is no surprise that in the fields of advertising and public relations, women also hold many of the top positions, as well as many of the specialized account executive and supervisory posts.

From our first day in business, John Adams Associates has always had a majority of women professionals. This is not because of any deliberate policy. We were too small to have personnel policies. We just didn't think in terms of gender. We had only two questions:

Can you do the job? And how soon can you start? Two of our first women executives were former colleagues in the government. Another was a former colleague from Congressional Quarterly. So I was already aware of their capabilities. We never had to advertise for staff. We had a steady stream of applicants. To the extent our finances would allow, we tried to give everyone a chance to get their foot on the ladder. Some started as interns and stayed on to become highly competent professionals and vice presidents.

At the time we started our firm, in the early seventies, most executives of public relations firms were men. Women were still largely relegated to the roles of secretaries, administrative assistants, or, at best, researchers to help the men. This was true throughout the business world and even among the supposedly enlightened media and broadcast networks. Yet women bring unique strengths to any company, as Lisa Gersh, the top executive of Martha Stewart Living Omnimedia, recently noted in an article in *The Economist* (July 23, 2011). She pointed out that, among other things, women are more collaborative than men and are better at multitasking. I could add a list of other qualities where I have seen them outshine male counterparts, to the great benefit of our firm and our clients.

One of our most notable successes was Barbara Bankoff, who came to us from Chicago via the Environmental Protection Agency. She was a brilliant government relations strategist with a quiet but engaging manner. Congressional staffers liked her personally and appreciated the fact that she was always well prepared. She was particularly skillful in marshaling persuasive facts in support of our clients' positions. In a single week, she convinced the editorial boards of the country's three most influential papers—*The New York Times*, *The Wall Street Journal*, and *The Washington Post*—to run simultaneous editorials opposing a bill that would have preserved a shipping monopoly, raising prices for shippers and consumers. The bill, about to be passed, was instantly withdrawn. Its promoters were stunned and wondered how it happened. In addition to handling a number of environmental issues—she was an expert on the Clean

Air Act—Barbara handled our Aerospatiale account, persuading lawmakers on Capitol Hill to support the Coast Guard's choice of a French helicopter, the Dauphin, over its American rivals. She also represented the Canadian company Bombardier, which had won the bidding to provide new subway cars for New York City. Only one American company made subway cars, and it predictably went crying to Congress against the purchase of these "foreign" products. A little research revealed, however, that this "all-American" company was actually German owned. With Barbara's help, Bombardier and New York City prevailed.

High Achievers

Another notable achiever was Pamela (Kostmayer) Whitney, a former staffer for Senator Ed Muskie, who was a creative genius.

The mother of two young girls, she helped persuade Chrysler to market the Plymouth Voyager as the ultimate child-safe family wagon, based on the new child-safety car-seat laws then being implemented at the state level throughout the country. Chrysler officials were so impressed by her knowledge and enthusiasm that they asked her to be their national spokesperson. She had the perfect personality for the task. As she did interview after interview on television and radio and with newspapers, the Voyager's sales soared. She also had a special gift for using imaginative visuals to promote legislation favoring our clients. The introduction of visuals to staid Capitol Hill press conferences was new and innovative at the time, and she was the unquestioned expert. In one case, to draw attention to anticounterfeiting legislation that had been mired in committee, she hired two wholesome-looking twins, dressed them identically, and used a six-foot graphic board to ask, "Which twin has the phony?" It was the lead story on all three networks, and the legislation soon passed with comfortable margins. On another occasion, on behalf of a group of undertakers, she had coffins carried up the Capitol steps—again ensuring network coverage and a legislative victory. Our firm became known—and still is—for our expertise in generating media support for legislative issues.

Carol Anderson, one of the few executives to join us from another public relations firm, added to this reputation. She was not only creative but also a great detail person, beloved by law firms looking for media to help their clients, because she quickly understood the nuances and was able to convey them in simple terms to the media, particularly editorial writers. For one major Chicago law firm, she developed so much publicity on the arcane issue of the taxation of intangible assets (such as goodwill) that we stopped the proposed tax legislation dead in its tracks.

We also came to be regarded as a great training ground for talent. The risk here was that clients would steal our people away, which sometimes happened. Monica Quagliotti, who handled our Range Rover account, was so good at her job that the company hired her away and eventually made her their West Coast marketing chief. Michelle Menchin, a former freelance journalist in Boston, came to us to start a career in public relations but was all too soon stolen away by the client she worked with, the consulting division of Coopers & Lybrand. Jennifer Swint came to us from Colorado, where she literally grew up on the ski slopes. Energetic, determined, and a great manager, she was a huge success in all aspects of our business and was eventually snapped up by one of the big New York firms. She became a top executive with Powell Tate (named for former White House communications chiefs Jody Powell and Sheila Tate) and ultimately APCO Worldwide, Washington's biggest and most successful public relations firm. These and other high achievers made us the envy of more than a few competitors.

We have often been asked the secret of our hiring policy. Many firms look for prior experience and give applicants writing or other tests. A typical question is, "Where do you expect to be in five years?" We considered such questions to be unfair to job seekers. We did not indulge in them. We hired people mostly on the basis of character and personality. We knew we could teach them what they needed to know about public relations. We also looked for a certain spark, a certain energy. A perfect example was Lori Rosen, a recent college graduate who had just returned from several weeks' working on a kibbutz in Israel. She had spent the day walking around Washington knocking on the doors of public relations firms, but without an appointment, she made little headway. When she arrived at our office late in the afternoon, she was obviously dead tired. As we began to talk, her first question was, "Do you mind if I take my shoes off? My feet are killing me." This somewhat untraditional start to a job interview told me everything I needed to know: she was honest, direct, unafraid—and she had a sense of humor. We hired her right away, and she was soon one of the stars of our team.

Lori eventually started her own very successful firm in New York City, The Rosen Group, and appeared in person on both the very first and very last broadcasts of *The Oprah Winfrey Show*, where she was also a star. We stay in touch, as we try to do with most of our alumnae.

Mr. Public Diplomacy
and the Famous "Kitchen Debate"

"Public diplomacy" is another one of those aspects of public relations or public affairs that means different things to different people.

My own introduction to it was the Amerika Haus in Munich, Germany, a quiet oasis from the busy world outside, where you could read American books and magazines, listen to occasional lectures or recitals, and even watch American movies. It was one of several such "America houses" around the world run by the United States Information Agency (USIA), an autonomous entity that officially represented America but was not involved in politics or traditional diplomacy. Its role was "public" diplomacy, defined by the State Department as "intended to inform or influence public opinion in other countries (through) publications, motion pictures, cultural exchanges, radio, and television." It was citizen-to-citizen rather than government-to-government.

To me, the person who has most personified this country's public diplomacy efforts is a former deputy director of USIA named Gilbert A. Robinson, once president of a major public relations firm in New York, who for half a century has brought his considerable experience, ideas, and immense energy to bear on improving the communications efforts of the U.S. government. He began this work as a junior official of the Commerce Department, assigned in 1956 to create and manage an American exhibit in Izmir, Turkey, followed almost immediately by an exhibit in Tunisia. He was then appointed coordinator of the American National Exhibition in Moscow in 1959, one of the largest and most important public diplomacy efforts ever undertaken. It was a true showcase of American ingenuity and consumer products, from the first color television to the latest autos and a model American kitchen. It was a huge success with the Russian people—more than sixty thousand visited in a single weekend—and it had a major influence on changing negative perceptions of the United States.

Today, the exhibition is mostly remembered for the famous Nixon-Khrushchev kitchen debate, a totally unplanned event orchestrated by Robinson with the help of an enterprising public relations man named Bill Safire, who was representing the model home. Robinson brought the two leaders together in the kitchen. They argued about which country's products were better, and they seemed to thoroughly enjoy themselves. The event made for huge headlines and photos around the world. The driving force behind this very successful exhibition was President Eisenhower, who was convinced that the United States needed to do a better job of communicating with the rest of the world at the citizen-to-citizen level.

Safire, of course, went on to be a gifted speechwriter for President Nixon and Vice President Agnew, creating Agnew's memorable phrase about the "nattering nabobs of negativism," before joining *The New York Times*, where he remained as a witty, influential, and highly successful political columnist for more than thirty years. He and Robinson remained close friends until Safire's untimely death in 2009. I have always felt grateful to Gil for introducing us. They were two of the most impressive and most gentlemanly people I ever had the privilege of knowing.

After a few years in private business in New York, where, among other things, he organized the first American business delegation to China, Gil was invited back to Washington to join the Reagan administration as the deputy director of USIA under Reagan family friend Charles Wick, who knew little about public relations, leaving most of the decisions to Robinson. In fact, Robinson was the first senior official in the USIA's history with a professional background in public relations.

One day, he received a phone call from President Reagan and Secretary of State Schultz on the phone together. They were not happy with the State Department's public diplomacy efforts, they told him, and wanted him to move over to State to help them improve. Schultz suggested he take three months to talk with various key people in the department and then offer his recommendations. After many interviews with senior career officials and political appointees, Robinson concluded that the problem was that most diplomats serving abroad, while very good at diplomacy, negotiations, and managing an embassy, did not have communicating with the citizens of their host country foremost in their thoughts. Nor did they have any training in how to use a radio microphone or, most importantly, how to conduct themselves in television interviews or presentations. They would make very good speeches, but not think much about media follow-up.

Robinson told Schultz that he should create an office in the State Department dedicated to public diplomacy and make it part of every diplomat's training. "Great," Schultz replied. "Will you be willing to head it up?"

"No," Robinson said. "I do not want to manage another bureaucracy—but I will be happy to act as an adviser." So Schultz appointed him his Special Adviser for Public Diplomacy with the rank of ambassador. He later commented that Robinson was "one of the most creative people I have ever worked with, in business or government."

Like Schultz, I came to know Robinson well over the years as a colleague, friend, and always wise counselor. I, too, was impressed by his creativity and his vision. He thought big. A good example was one of his first recommendations to Schultz. "I would like to pull together all our ambassadors in Europe," he said. "Bring them to London. They need to learn simple things like how to speak into the camera and speak in short sentences." He recommended the use of a professional trainer from one of the large public relations firms. He then arranged for a reporter from the British Broadcasting Corporation to interview each of the ambassadors. The following day, the reporter delivered his critique of the interviews. Instead of being offended or embarrassed, the ambassadors loved it. The whole event was considered a great success, and TV training is now part of every ambassador's preparation before assuming a post abroad.

In 1999, the USIA was merged into the State Department, ostensibly for financial reasons, but primarily to satisfy the political priorities of Senator Jesse Helms, the conservative North Carolina Republican and powerful chairman of the Senate Foreign Relations Committee. Secretary of State Madeleine Albright, anxious not to offend Helms, went along with the merger. Many foreign policy experts, including Robinson, were disappointed with this outcome.

After all these years, Robinson continues to run his international consulting business in Washington, advising government officials and business executives on trade, government relations, and communications issues. One of his principal clients is the American Chamber of Commerce in Russia (AmCham Russia), which represents some 750 American companies doing business in Russia, including most of the Fortune 500. Robinson also founded and has for years supported a significant charity in that country to feed and clothe Russian orphans.

A Lifetime Love Affair

My love affair with journalism began when I was very young and has continued throughout my life. I still thrill to the names of newspapers like the *Ticonderoga Sentinel,* which I discovered while driving through the Green Mountains of Vermont, and the *Bloomington Pantagraph*, where the famous *Washington Post* columnist David Broder began his career, and the *Wapakoneta Daily News,* the Ohio hometown newspaper of astronaut Neil Armstrong.

Local papers do far more than tell you the news. They reflect the culture and standards and concerns of their communities. They record the activities of their schools, councils, and Kiwanis and the births, weddings, and deaths that define the passage of generations. They carry ads for everything you could need, from real estate agents to hardware stores, from plumbers to cleaning services. Readers relate to their local papers in ways they will never relate to the Internet. Experts say that "traditional" media today simply cannot compete with the fast-evolving digital offerings of the Internet. While this is increasingly and sadly true, I would argue that, conversely, the Internet in all its variety simply cannot compete with the public service provided by local papers and their reporters and editors, who love their communities and know every inch of their territory.

The traditional media have chronicled our lives and the great events of our time since the invention of the printing press and the microphone. All our great journalists, from Zenger to Reston and Murrow to Cronkite, learned their trade and achieved their greatest triumphs in the traditional media. They have served us well.

Today, the media scene is changing so fast that no one knows what journalism will look like in a few years, or even next year. It may well be all electronic with no newspapers at all. But it is probably fair to assume that there will always be a role for journalists as long as there is news to convey and people want an honest, independent version of events, as surely they always will in a democratic society. Indeed, it is difficult to imagine how a democracy can survive without this kind of journalism, regardless of the means of delivery.

So despite the many uncertainties hanging over the profession, and the serious economic problems caused for newspapers by the growth of the Internet—which has forced many publications out of business and required journalists to find other ways to earn a living—I would still urge young people to seriously consider journalism as a career. Why? Because, for you as a journalist, the world is your oyster. There is no limit to what you can do, where you can go, and what you can report on. You have an independence that few other professions can offer. It is a wonderfully liberating experience. And it is a continuing education process: you are always learning something new.

The bottom line for those considering journalism as a career is that the Internet badly needs you. Today, it needs reporters and editors with the traditional journalistic skills for assessing the realities of a situation, for ferreting out the truth and making it comprehensible to an ever widening audience. As the Internet expands, its need for people with journalistic training will expand with it, though that training will inevitably evolve to accommodate the differing needs of the new medium. Without this journalistic discipline, the Internet would seem destined to become simply another Tower of Babel, with thousands, even millions of so-called citizen-journalists writing whatever they feel like writing, asserting all kinds of "truths" that have little or no basis in fact.

Our firm, like many others, monitors the Internet closely, twenty-four hours a day, for information that might be important to our clients. We find we have to spend a great deal of time analyzing, explaining, and otherwise correcting many of these "news" items because they are simply wrong or seriously misleading. Often they are just ideologies or prejudices dressed up as news. Another problem with the Internet as a source of news is that once the misleading information is posted, there is no realistic way of undoing the damage. Some sites allow comments for a limited period. Others do not allow any form of correction. Whether this is deliberate or not, the absence of a rigorous correcting mechanism seems terribly unfair to the millions of younger people who today have come to rely on the Internet as their chief source of information.

The British weekly newsmagazine *The Economist* ran a cover story on "the future of news" in its issue of July 9, 2011. Its theme was that professional journalism is irrevocably on its way out and the future will belong to the millions of citizen-journalists, gossip-mongers, activists, nonprofit groups, and other self-appointed experts who increasingly dominate the Internet. It argued that this new diversity of sources would not necessarily be a bad thing, because it would be largely self-correcting. At the same time, it acknowledged that "in a world where millions of new sources are emerging on the Internet, consumers are overwhelmed with information and want to be told what it all means." This seemed to make the case for an important future Internet role for the professional journalist as writer, editor, analyst, and explainer-in-chief. I feel this need will only increase and that journalists and journalism students should make sure they stake their rightful claim. The opportunities are there.

Lessons Learned

After a fairly long life in the trenches of journalism and public affairs, I am at times asked what lessons I have learned. It is tempting to be flip, but I will try to be serious, beginning with the matter of trust. "Never trust anyone over thirty" was a phrase popular in the sixties and seventies. The sad fact is that trust of anyone in authority has largely broken down in the United States, Britain, and other major nations, and this dynamic is seriously undermining our society and democratic processes. It is a key reason for the present dysfunctional state of governance in the Western world. It also has been a major factor in the disruption of our financial systems. It is a dangerous trend, and I do not know how it can be easily reversed.

Scientific research is perhaps the most critical area where trust has been lost. The cause here seems to be the deliberate fudging of data in order to qualify for greater levels of funding. Most leading professional journals have been victimized by researchers presenting falsified results. This is an especially alarming trend in the field of medical research, where fraudulent results can put lives at stake. Revered professional publications ranging from *The New England Journal of Medicine* to Britain's *Lancet* have been among the victims. They say they simply do not have the resources to undertake the necessary supervision, and that today's "peer reviewers" do not have or do not take the time to conduct adequate reviews. The problem is compounded by the ever-increasing number of studies applying for an ever-increasing flow of funds.

On a lighter note, I have noticed over the years that those who confidently make predictions are usually wrong. This would seem to apply especially to economists and political pundits. The late *New York Times* columnist James Reston used to write an annual column citing all the predictions of the previous year that had not come true. These were usually predictions of bad things that never came to pass, so it was always encouraging to read and sometimes quite hilarious.

Perhaps the one lesson I have learned above all others is the incredible influence that a single individual can have on the course of events, or in the popular political parlance, to "make a difference." The most obvious recent examples are in the field of computer technology, where Bill Gates of Microsoft and the late Steve Jobs of Apple totally changed the world of communications and improved the lives of millions the world over.

In the 1980s, the Polish shipyard worker Lech Walesa, who later became president of Poland, led his fellow workers in defying his country's communist regime, creating the Solidarity movement that led to the defeat of communism in Poland, throughout Eastern Europe, and eventually in the Soviet Union itself. In short, he brought the Cold War to an end without a shot being fired.

It was also in the 1980s that the late Charlie Wilson, the John Wayne–like congressman from Texas, convinced Congress to support the largest covert operation in CIA history in order to drive the Russians out of Afghanistan. The story of his extraordinary achievement was told by George Crile in the book *Charlie Wilson's War*, and in the movie of the same name in which Tom Hanks played the role of Wilson.

Jack Grayson, the dynamic university professor who was selected to head the price control program during the Nixon administration, overcame numerous bureaucratic roadblocks to turn an unpopular program into a major success. His Price Commission became one of the most innovative and effective agencies in the federal government. He then established the country's first think tank to focus on improving productivity, setting standards adopted throughout the world. In his eighties, he developed ways of transferring productivity processes from the business world to the field of education.

In the world of finance, Jack Bogle literally revolutionized the mutual fund industry by creating index funds to reduce costs and improve returns for millions of small investors. Despite initial skepticism and even ridicule from Wall Street, which did not want to lose its commissions, Bogle's Vanguard group of index funds, with hundreds of billions in assets, has been one of the financial industry's greatest success stories.

Reg Green was a financial journalist whose seven-year-old son, Nicholas, was shot by bandits while the family was on vacation in Italy. Doctors pronounced him brain dead and asked Reg and his wife, Maggie, to consider donating his organs—a rarity at the time in Italy. They agreed, giving new life to seven young Italians. Their humanitarian gesture garnered international attention and led to a vast increase in organ and tissue donations in Italy and around the world. Reg wrote of this experience in a much-acclaimed book, *The Nicholas Effect*, followed later by a book on the experience of giving and receiving organ transplants through the eyes of those involved, *The Gift that Heals*. In articles, speeches, and interviews he, his wife and their daughter, Eleanor, have contributed hugely to the understanding of organ and tissue donation throughout the world, saving and transforming many thousands of lives—an ongoing living memorial to a much-loved son.

In the often controversial field of education, Susan Patrick, a former head of educational technology at the Department of Education, has been a pioneer and tireless advocate for online learning for K-12 students. From a standing start, her organization, the International Association for K-12 Online Learning, now has nearly four thousand members. More than 80 percent of school districts in America now offer online learning. The figures will undoubtedly be higher by the time you read this. Her goal is to ensure that all students, whatever their circumstances, have access to a world-class education through online learning, customized to each student's needs. She believes that the future of education is in personalized digital learning for every student. "It is happening around the world. We have to make it happen in the United States," she says. We are sure she will succeed. Susan is one of the most dynamic and determined individuals I have ever known.

These are but a few examples of the countless others out there who are truly making a difference, who are making things happen for the better in every walk of life and who are selflessly improving the lives of others. It has been a great lesson to know they are there and inspiring to know some of them personally. It also confirms my belief that despite all the miraculous advances in technology in recent years, from communications to space travel, everything in the end depends on the character, beliefs and relationships of individuals.

Undoubtedly the greatest example of one person making a difference in my own lifetime is the late Winston Churchill, who was sixty-five years old when he became Britain's prime minister in World War II, at a time when many of his contemporaries, to their shame, were ready to surrender to the seemingly invincible military might of Nazi Germany. Many European countries had already surrendered, and American politicians were not at all sure that the United States should get involved. Against all odds, Churchill rallied the British people and their allies throughout the world to resist and eventually defeat the Nazi war machine. Although much has been written on the subject, including several classic volumes by Churchill himself, I feel it is good to occasionally remind ourselves of the magnificence of this one man's achievement. And to recall, too, that much of his formidable character came from his American mother, Jenny Jerome, a native of Brooklyn, New York.

One shudders to think how different the world might be today if he had not lived.

Epilogue

One of the great challenges of writing memoirs is deciding what to include and what to leave out. In this volume, I have tried to focus on what would be of most interest to the reader—particularly younger readers considering journalism or public relations as a career. In doing so, I have inevitably overlooked a number of events and people who were and are important and probably should have been included. I have no excuse, except an imperfect memory and the pressures of time. Following are a few examples of what Catholics might refer to as these sins of omission. They are a few of many.

I had the good fortune to work for many years on a number of different issues with a brilliant public relations man named Bill Baker.

Bill was almost certainly the most creative automotive public relations and marketing man of the last quarter century in both Europe and the United States. He was the one who put Britain's Range Rover on the map with a famous series of expeditions through Middle Eastern deserts and Latin American forests. Auto writers loved him, not least for his ever-present wit and good humor. He enjoyed the fact that most of these rugged, go-anywhere, permanent four-wheel drive vehicles were sold not in places like Colorado or California, but in the manicured suburbs of Connecticut, where they seldom went anywhere. In another capacity, as vice president of communications for Sony Corporation of America, he helped launch the Walkman and orchestrated Sony's successful campaign to prevent Hollywood from imposing copyright taxes on VCRs and videotapes.

Clint McCarty, an old friend from CBS days, was one of the most graceful writers I ever knew. After leaving John Adams Associates, where he wrote mostly on environmental issues, he researched and wrote a much-acclaimed book on the social and political history of his home state, Alabama, focusing in particular on the shifts in political power in the relatively impoverished Wilcox County, where he was born. *The Reins of Power* is a must-read for anyone interested in the real-world effects of the civil rights movement in the South.

Roger Allan, another graceful writer, former newspaperman, and public relations executive, became a novelist in his spare time, beginning with a gripping murder mystery at Virginia's celebrated Homestead resort, *These Mountains Have Secrets*. Roger knew the area and its people well, having worked on the local paper and as public relations director of the Homestead. It's another "must-read," particularly for those with an affinity for that part of the world—Virginia, West Virginia and its densely wooded mountains, and this historic resort.

Others among the many I should have mentioned are Jean Young, one of the most capable public relations people I ever met, who did great work for us before starting her own successful firm, Young and Associates, specializing in technical issues; Beverly Jackson and Jim Elliott, two superb media relations professionals who were part of our original team of former Price Commission colleagues; and Caroline Herbert (now Caroline Lewis) who, among other clients, handled the renowned Gow School in upstate New York, a prep school for dyslexic boys, which proved highly educational for all of us.

In addition to John Heinze and Ann Crampton, both mentioned earlier, the current very efficient team at John Adams Associates includes such media and public affairs experts as vice president Michelle Kincaid, who leads our cybersecurity practice, and senior vice president Francie Israeli, a talented manager, writer, and counselor. Another longtime vice president, Rachna Sethi, brought us all a greater appreciation of India, with its incredible history, customs, style, disciplines, strong family relationships—and exquisite food.

In 2009, we merged with the Kellen Company, an international association management and professional services firm, which brought us additional offices and staff in New York, Brussels and Beijing.

As I look back over my own life in journalism, public affairs, and public relations, I feel truly grateful for the opportunities that have come my way and the great people I have known and worked with. Perhaps the highlight was working for Radio Free Europe in Germany with so many members of the "greatest generation," who had fought against and suffered under both Nazism and Communism. Later, it was a true privilege to know and work with the leaders of Poland's famous Solidarity movement, who literally brought the Soviet Union to its knees. These were stirring times. It was great, as a young journalist, to be part of such historic developments.

As the songwriter put it, "Life is a cabaret, old chum." It has been for me. There have been very few dull moments. I know I have been lucky and only hope I may have done some good along the way.

As the Irish writer Robert Lynd said at the conclusion of one of his essays: "It's an interesting world. I'm glad I didn't miss it."

Appendices

1. Op-eds

One of the most important services a public affairs firm provides to clients is the drafting and placement of articles of opinion, usually referred to as "opinion pieces," which, if accepted, appear on the page opposite the editorial page, and hence are called op-eds.

These appendices include three examples of op-eds of which we are particularly proud:

"Thank You, America," an article by Jan Nowak that we edited and placed in *The Washington Post* and the *International Herald Tribune*.

"Chechnya Will Never Surrender," an article by a leader of the free Chechens, Khozh-Ahmed Noukhaev, which we helped draft and place in *The Wall Street Journal*.

"Let's Talk Trash," a more recent article by Bruce Parker, president of the National Solid Wastes Management Association, that was carried by some thirty dailies with a total circulation of 2.5 million.

2. Advertorials

We also include three examples of what are termed *advertorials*, which are advertisements written to convey information of importance to the client, in this case The Gold Institute. These are three of a series of advertorials, whose purpose was to inform opinion leaders—including the media—of the many essential uses of gold in today's world. They appeared in *The New York Times* and other major papers.

"Strengthening America"

"The Healing Power of Gold"

"A Golden Age of Technology."

Op-Eds

Thank You, America

By: Jan Nowak
The Washington Post

This July 4, many Americans may feel baffled and disappointed by the waves of anti-Americanism sweeping through countries that, not too long ago, were either saved or helped by the United States. Allies such as France and Great Britain and former enemies such as Germany and Japan benefited greatly from America's generosity and support in their time of need, as did Belgium, Holland, Italy, Russia, Poland, South Korea, and the Philippines, Taiwan, and others. Without the United States, some of these countries may no longer exist.

Those of us who remember and remain grateful should no longer remain silent. For people like me—and there are millions of us—this Fourth of July is a good opportunity to say, "Thank you, America."

My old country, Poland, is a good example. I was born eighty-nine years ago on the eve of World War I in Warsaw, when Poles were forced to live under the despotic rule of the Russian czars. In 1917 Woodrow Wilson made the restoration of Polish independence one of his fourteen conditions for peace. If it had not been for Wilson, Poland might have disappeared forever from the map of Europe. The United States did not have any strategic or economic interests in this remote eastern part of the European continent. But thanks to America, the ambitions of the Hohenzollern Empire to dominate all of Europe were thwarted.

The war in Poland did not end in 1918, however. For six more years, the wheels of war rolled over the Polish countryside as Poles fought to repel the invasions of the Red Army. The country was left in ruins. Food was scarce. The undernourished population was hit by epidemics of typhoid and Spanish flu.

I belong to the generation of children in this era, the early 1920s, who were saved by the benevolent intervention of the United States, in the person of the future president Herbert Hoover. As a private citizen, Hoover organized the emergency supplies of food, medicine, and clothing that saved a starving and sick nation. I still remember the tin boxes inscribed, "American Relief Committee for Poland."

The Polish state survived, but with no economic resources, no reserves of gold or foreign currencies. Roaring inflation had brought the country to the verge of collapse. The United States came forward once again, providing the Dillon loans, which helped stabilize the Polish economy.

Following the surrender of France in 1940, Hitler was only one step from victory. The United States, by joining Great Britain as it faced alone the greater might of Nazi Germany, and at enormous sacrifice of young American lives, saved European civilization and its values. It is known that Hitler's postwar plans called for elimination of Poland's educated classes, while the rest of the population were to become slave workers. Once again, the United States saved the lives of millions. I am grateful to have been one of them.

Tragically, the defeat of Nazi Germany did not bring freedom to the nations of east and central Europe. Hitler's tyranny was replaced by Stalin's terror. It was the United States that contained the Soviet Union's drive for domination of Europe. It understood before others that the Cold War would be a struggle for human minds.

One of its major weapons in this war was the skillful use of radio. As a former radio operator with the Polish underground and later a broadcaster with the BBC Foreign Service, I was recruited in the early 1950s to start the Polish service of Radio Free Europe (RFE). No country but the United States would launch or could have launched such an ambitious undertaking, broadcasting from dawn to midnight.

RFE destroyed the monopoly of the Communist public media and frustrated the efforts of the Soviet Union to isolate the satellite countries from the outside world. Citizens of these countries had only to tune in to the RFE frequency to learn what their governments

171

were attempting to hide from them. People were able to get the information they needed to form their own views, even if they could not speak them. Their minds remained free.

Workers' strikes were banned under communism. So when Polish shipyard workers in Gdansk, led by Lech Walesa, defiantly called a strike in August 1980, the government immediately ordered a news blackout. But within hours, the whole country knew of the workers' resistance and related developments from RFE broadcasts. Because the Communists feared a general strike might follow, they quickly agreed to a compromise settlement with the shipyard workers. Solidarity was born.

The following year, however, the Communist leader, Gen. Wojciech Jaruzelski, sought to destroy the movement by imposing martial law. The United States responded by applying a sophisticated carrot-and-stick policy in which Jaruzelski was never forced into a position where he had nothing to lose and nothing to gain. Economic sanctions were imposed, but economic assistance was promised. The patient and consistent application of this policy over the next eight years resulted in the survival of Solidarity, which emerged triumphant in 1989.

News of this victory spread rapidly to East Berlin, Prague, Budapest, Bucharest, and Sofia, as well as Moscow, through the broadcasts of RFE, Radio Liberty, RIAS (Radio in the American Sector, Berlin), and the Voice of America. The overthrow of Poland's communist dictatorship inspired millions throughout the Soviet orbit, unleashing an avalanche that brought down the Berlin Wall and led to the reunification of Germany, the self-liberation of the nations of east-central Europe, and eventually the disintegration of the Soviet Union.

Poland formed the first non-communist government in the former Soviet empire. But the nation's economy remained a disaster area. Again the United States came to the rescue. Poland's first democratic government and the nation's economy were saved by U.S. leadership in proposing and aggressively promoting an emergency international financial assistance package.

In the spring of 1998, I watched from the public gallery of the U.S. Senate as it ratified the admission into NATO of Poland, Hungary, and the Czech Republic. For the first time in its history, my old country was not only free but also secure.

Thank you, America.

(July 3, 2002)

Chechnya Will Never Surrender

By: Khozh-Ahmed Noukhaev
The Wall Street Journal

Just why are 100,000 Russian troops, supported by bombers, heavy artillery, and tanks, trying to demolish Grozny, the capital of Chechnya, my homeland? Why is it so important for Russia to smash into pieces this tiny country in the Caucasus Mountains a thousand miles from Moscow? Many in the West must wonder: Who are these "rebels and bandits" the Russians say they are fighting?

Let me tell you, for I am one of them. We are the Chechen people. Men, women, and children. We are called "rebels" by Moscow because we want to be free to govern ourselves. We have been fighting for our independence from Russia ever since Ivan the Terrible tried to invade our land over four hundred years ago. And like other former Soviet republics, we declared our sovereignty when the Soviet Union collapsed in 1991.

It is true that there are still some lawless elements in our country, as there are in most countries of the former Soviet Union and most notably in Russia itself. But this does not justify what the Russians are doing today: the wholesale destruction of a country and its people. There are more bandits in Moscow than in the whole of Chechnya.

The first thing to understand is that we Chechens are not Russians. We were invaded by Russia, first by the czars and then by the Bolsheviks. In 1944 Joseph Stalin began what is now called *ethnic cleansing*—driving virtually the whole population of Chechnya thousands of miles into the Soviet wilderness.

Like most other Chechens, I eventually returned to my homeland. We have a deep love for our country, our culture, and our traditions. We are a friendly people. But we are also fiercely independent. We do not take easily to being pushed around or invaded by foreigners.

When we declared our independence in 1991, it was because we wanted to be free. Free to elect our own leaders and make our own decisions. Free to make our own alliances. Free to live our own lives. And free to profess the faith of our fathers on our fathers' land.

As the world now knows, this did not sit well with certain Russian leaders, especially the military, who didn't care about democracy and who strongly resented the loss of their empire and their authority. So in 1994 they invaded little Chechnya again, to bring us in line, to "teach us a lesson." It would, they thought, be a quick victory—and a warning to the other republics.

Instead, despite their vastly superior numbers and armor, they suffered heavy casualties and were driven back, eventually signing an agreement granting Chechnya its independence for five years, during which time our future relations were to be negotiated.

It was a terribly costly war, especially for our civilian population. Thousands of our children were killed or mutilated. But by 1996 we were at least free again, and we set about the task of rebuilding our country. We began with hospitals and mosques, for Russia had destroyed them all.

The Russians never honored the peace agreement they signed with us in 1996, and they never negotiated in good faith on our future relations, as the treaty had called for. Instead, as we now know, they were just biding their time, looking for an excuse to return in greater force. The Russian generals who were humbled by their defeat in 1995 are now back in charge of destroying Chechnya.

This time, it is reported, they insisted on having total authority to do as they sought fit—to allow their troops to convert Chechnya into a death camp, with no interference from Moscow politicians. Since they began their new invasion in September, Russia's soldiers have run amok. A quarter of the Chechen people have been driven from their homes.

But once again, Russia has miscalculated. Despite a huge increase in troops and armaments and a withering bombardment from the air, the Russians have been unable to reassert their authority in

Chechnya, and as I write this, they have still been unable to take the capital, Grozny. Their first attempt to enter the city with tanks ended in a humiliating defeat. Other defeats will surely follow.

And even if the Russians succeed in demolishing Grozny and installing a quisling government, they still will not have won. As Winston Churchill once asked in a similar situation, "What sort of people do they think we are?" Chechens will never surrender to the Russians. We will continue the fight, one way or another, until our country is again free and independent, however long it may take.

If the Russians were smart, they would understand this. They would halt further unnecessary casualties among their young, poorly trained soldiers, force their generals to swallow their pride and begin to negotiate peace. Otherwise Chechnya will become a worse quagmire for them than Afghanistan, which led to the breakup of the Soviet Union. With endless guerrilla warfare, subjecting the Russian military to endless casualties and endless humiliation, Chechnya could well trigger the breakup of the Russian Federation.

Russia clearly cannot afford this. It has nothing to gain by staying in Chechnya. It should cut its losses and save what face it can by negotiating a new peace agreement now. This time, however, an international commission should be created to make sure Russia honors that agreement. For both Europe and the United States have a vital strategic and economic interest in restoring peace to the Caucasus as soon as possible—before the war in Chechnya spills over to Georgia, Azerbaijan, and the vast Caspian oil fields.

(December 27, 1999)

On Earth Day, Let's Talk Trash

By Bruce J. Parker

The fortieth anniversary of Earth Day is an excellent opportunity to talk trash.

Let's face it. Americans often get flak for producing too much garbage. EPA estimates that we threw out over 250 million tons of garbage in the last year alone.

Put those numbers into context, however, and you will find that we are doing a lot better than we were a few decades ago. In fact, proper waste management is actually one of America's greatest environmental successes. In the last two decades alone, we have witnessed a startling transformation in how we deal with all the garbage.

Consider this: while the waste stream has increased over the years along with the population, we actually sent over seven million tons *less* waste to disposal than we did almost twenty years ago. That is precisely because we've gotten better at using trash as a resource.

Take recycling—a major environmental achievement. Curbside recycling programs were virtually unheard of twenty years ago, but today, such programs have helped to more than double America's recycling rate since 1990.

Meanwhile, manufacturers have found that recycled materials cost less than virgin, and that that their use saves a substantial amount of energy and natural resources. Aluminum cans are a great example. Manufacturing one pound of aluminum from recycled material requires only 4 percent of the energy needed to make virgin aluminum from its basic starting mineral, bauxite ore.

Waste-based energy is another major transformation. The Energy Department reports that more than half of America's renewable energy comes from our trash—more than the energy outputs from solar, hydroelectric, and wind power combined. Millions of homes and businesses, including major companies like Honeywell and Dell, are powered by clean, renewable fuel generated using by-products of our garbage at waste-to-energy and landfill-gas-to-energy plants.

The use of waste-based energy reduces our reliance on fossil fuels, and helps to address global warming. EPA estimates that waste-based energy projects are saving more than 270 million barrels of oil a year—the equivalent of eliminating air pollution from 27 million cars.

Even our landfills are better. Once little more than open-air pits, today's modern landfills are state-of-the-art facilities, carefully regulated and managed to reduce air pollution, control leachate, and minimize odors.

After they've reached capacity, engineers and landscape designers turn the landfills into golf courses, wildlife refuges, and other green spaces. One of the largest former landfills in the country—Fresh Kills in New York City—is currently being developed into a large urban park three times the size of the city's famous Central Park.

While Americans can certainly be proud of these achievements, we're not stopping here. Local authorities and solid waste companies are now working together to figure out how to shrink the pile even further.

Many cities are turning to "zero waste" programs. "Zero waste" doesn't mean "no waste," but rather encourages Americans to reduce, reuse, and recycle what they throw away, and for manufacturers and others in the supply chain to find new uses for the stuff we once threw away. As part of the effort, trash companies are consulting with major retailers like Walmart to cut down on packaging waste and are working with government officials to improve the efficiency of recycling programs.

Of course the transition to a "zero waste" society won't be easy or quick, but we're getting closer than ever before—thanks to a deeper respect for Mother Earth, technological innovation, and the realization that today's waste is tomorrow's resource.

Bruce J. Parker is president and CEO of the National Solid Wastes Management Association in Washington, D.C.

This op-ed was carried in 2010 by approximately thirty daily papers with a total circulation of more than 2.5 million.

(April 22, 2011)

Advertorials

Strengthening America

Gold has been good to America. This ancient metal, the first used by man and still prized above all others, today plays a more vital role in the life and health of our nation than ever before.

Gold has become essential in today's high-tech world. It ensures the proper functioning of the most sensitive electronic instruments. In national defense. In telecommunications. In advanced biomedical research. In many other ways that ensure our health and safety at home, at work, on the road, and in the air.

The Pentagon specifies gold for critical instruments that may make the difference between life and death. Gold circuitry helped save the life of Air Force Captain Scott O'Grady when his plane was shot from the skies over Bosnia. NASA specifies gold for sensitive spacecraft instruments to ensure the safety of astronauts. Air traffic controllers depend on gold for the flawless operation of radar equipment around the clock.

On our nation's roads, hundreds of lives are saved and thousands of serious injuries prevented each year by the gold circuits in electronic sensors that ensure airbags operate without fail.

Gold is used in all these technologies because of its unmatched reliability. It is not affected by extremes of heat, cold, or damp. It does not rust, tarnish, or corrode. It remains a superior conductor of electricity under all circumstances. It is amazingly flexible. And it is virtually indestructible.

Gold has been good to America in many other ways. The extraction of gold from otherwise barren rock formations has created tens of thousands of well-paid jobs, not only in the West but in forty-six other states that make the modern equipment needed to find and extract gold more efficiently, more precisely, and with less disturbance to the natural environment. For every million dollars' worth of gold produced, the local economy grows by nearly $2 million and household earnings increase over $500,000.

Gold has been especially good to our national economy. As

recently as 1980, most of our gold had to be imported. Today, because of new technologies, we are able to produce domestically all the gold needed for defense, communications, aviation, medical research, computers, automobile safety, and other important applications.

Gold also generates billions of dollars of income for other industries throughout the United States. Each year, gold production contributes hundreds of millions in state and local taxes to fund roads, schools, hospitals, universities, and other facilities. It also provides over $500 million a year to the federal treasury. And it strengthens America's balance of trade by providing over $1.5 billion a year in exports.

The development of our modern, high-tech gold industry is an American success story. It has made our country stronger, more independent, and more competitive in the global marketplace. And in many unseen ways, it has made life better, healthier, and safer for millions of people here and throughout the world.

This advertorial was written for The Gold Institute and appeared in *The New York Times* and other major papers.

(1995 – 1997)

The Healing Power of Gold

In medieval Europe, alchemists mixed powdered gold into drinks to "comfort sore limbs," one of the earliest references to arthritis.

Word of gold's power to relieve the pain of arthritis passed down through the centuries. Its mysterious efficacy has been confirmed by modern medical research. Today it is widely used, in combination with other compounds, in the treatment of rheumatoid arthritis.

In ancient Rome, gold salves were used for the treatment of skin ulcers. Today, gold leaf plays an important role in the treatment of chronic ulcers.

As long as 4,500 years ago, the Egyptians used gold in dentistry. Remarkable examples of the artistry of these orthodontists have been found, perfectly preserved, by archaeologists of our own time. Today, American dentists use some thirteen tons of gold each year for crowns, bridges, inlays, and dentures. The reason? Gold is nontoxic, it can be shaped easily, and it is tough—it never wears, corrodes, or tarnishes.

The use of gold in modern medicine began around 1890, when the distinguished German bacteriologist Robert Koch discovered that compounds made with gold inhibited growth of the bacillus that caused tuberculosis. His work was honored with the Nobel Prize in Medicine.

Today, medical uses of gold have expanded greatly. It is used in surgery to patch damaged blood vessels, nerves, bones, and membranes. And it is used in the treatment of several forms of cancer. Injection of microscopic gold pellets helps retard prostate cancer in men. Women with ovarian cancer are treated with colloidal gold. And gold vapor lasers help seek out and destroy cancerous cells without harming their healthy neighbors.

Gold has become an important biomedical tool for scientists studying why the body behaves as it does. By attaching a molecular marker to a microscopic piece of gold, scientists can follow its movement through the body. And because gold is readily visible under an electron microscope, scientists now, for the first time, can see whether and where a reaction takes place in an individual cell.

Some researchers are placing gold on DNA to study the hybrid genetic material in cells. Others are using it to determine how cells respond to toxins, heat, and physical stress.

Because it is biologically benign, biochemists use gold to form compounds with proteins to create new lifesaving drugs. One experimental new gold compound blocks virus replication in infected cells. It is being tested for the treatment of AIDS.

Every day, surgeons use gold instruments to clear coronary arteries, and gold-coated lasers literally give new life to patients with once inoperable heart conditions and tumors.

Around the world, the unique qualities of gold are helping millions live longer, healthier, and more productive lives. One day, it might save your life.

This advertorial was written for The Gold Institute and appeared in *The New York Times* and other major papers.

(1995 – 1997)

A Golden Age of Technology

By any measure, we live in a golden age of technology. An age in which orbiting satellites tell us the temperature of the earth and measure the gaps in the ozone layer. An age in which a student can access all the works in the Library of Congress at the touch of a computer key. An age in which technology has increased the quality of millions of lives the world over.

This is a *golden age* not only because of the breathless pace of progress but because one of the major elements that has made this progress possible is gold itself. Once considered a luxury, this ancient metal has become a vital part of today's most advanced electronics, communications, medical sciences—and national security.

Soon after World War II, gold was used by American physicists to develop the world's first transistor, giving birth to modern electronics. A generation later, it was used to create the first microchip. Today, gold is integral to the reliable functioning of virtually all consumer electronics, from telephones, televisions, and VCRs to cameras, CDs, and personal computers. Every time you touch a computer key it strikes a gold circuit that relays your command to the computer's microprocessor.

In space, gold ensures the reliable working of the sophisticated electronics of manned spacecraft and weather and communications satellites. The lifeline that tethers an astronaut when he walks in space is coated with gold to protect it from thermal damage. Gold-covered visors protect astronauts' eyes. The space vehicles themselves are sheathed in gold foil to protect them from solar radiation.

Gold's extraordinary reflective power is used in defense to deflect and confuse the signals of heat-seeking missiles. The president's plane, Air Force One, is among the aircraft protected by gold's antimissile reflectors.

In modern astronomy, gold plays a vital role because of its

unmatched ability to reflect infrared light. Gold is used on the reflective mirrors of the world's largest twin telescopes, at the Keck Observatory in Hawaii, enabling astronomers to record the faintest emissions of light from the outer reaches of the universe.

Some of the most exciting uses of gold technology have been in medical science, from ensuring the reliability of lifesaving pacemakers to the effectiveness of lasers that have revolutionized surgery. It is used in the treatment of several forms of cancer. A gold compound that blocks virus replication in infected cells is being tested for the treatment of AIDS. By attaching a molecular marker to a microscopic piece of gold, scientists can detect whether and where a reaction takes place in an individual cell. Every day, surgeons use gold instruments to clear coronary arteries and literally give new life to patients with once inoperable heart conditions.

Whenever lives depend on the flawless operation of electronic equipment—in aircraft, in automobiles, in home security systems, and in virtually all military equipment, from nuclear submarines to space stations—gold technology is specified. This is because of its superior conductivity, unequaled reliability, and virtual indestructibility. It never rusts or corrodes and is unaffected by extremes of temperature. This is why gold has become such an essential component of today's rapidly expanding "high-tech" world. At the same time, it has become one of the country's most important natural resources.

This advertorial was written for The Gold Institute and appeared in *The New York Times* and other major papers.

(1995 – 1997)

Acknowledgments

Where does one start? This volume covers three quarters of a century. I am immensely grateful to the individuals who literally saved my life on so many occasions; to my dedicated elementary and secondary schoolteachers who spurred my interest in history and my curiosity about the world; to my role models in the military, journalism, and government who taught me so much about what Lord Avebury called *The Use of Life*; to my parents for their unlimited love; to my clients and colleagues at John Adams Associates over the past four decades for their friendship and support, enabling us all to prosper; and good friends such as Andy Alexander, Tom Buckmaster, Reg Green, and Llewellyn King for taking the time to read and greatly improve earlier versions. I am especially grateful to my wife, Judy, my daughter, Caroline, my brother, Wilf, and my cousin, Patricia, for their kind encouragement and helpful suggestions from the very beginning.

Index

Page numbers containing italic *"ph"* indicate photograph on page

E

Earth Day, 177–179
Eastern Europe
    communist governments of, 46
    Worldcom in, 111–112
Eaton Hall (Cheshire, England),
    14–15, 39, 99*ph*
The Economist (magazine)
    on the future of news, 157
    on women and men in the
        workplace, 146
editors, at Radio Free Europe (RFE),
    (Munich), 47
Edson, Andrew, 111
education, journalism career, 7
Edwards, Douglas, 77
Egypt, 24
Egyptians, using gold in dentistry, 184
Eisenhower, Dwight D., 42, 73, 152
Elizabeth, Queen (Queen Mother),
    15–16
Elizabeth II, Queen, x, 8–9
Elliott, Jim, 164
Elliott, Osborn, 92
Elmcrest Psychiatric Institute, 136–138
England. *See also* Great Britain;
    London
    Communist Party in, 11
    discovery of medieval wall
        paintings in Piccotts End, 9
    Eaton Hall (Cheshire), 14–15
    Hemel Hempstead, 4–5
    preparation for WWII, 1–2
    Royal Horse Guards barracks
        (Aldershot), 39
    School of Infantry (Warminster), 15
    schools during WWII, 3–4
    shooting range incident at Bisley, 38
    start of, 2–3
European Union, Poland as member
    of, 112

evacuation, of children during WWII,
    3
Exxon, 130–133
Exxon Valdez (supertanker), accident
    of, 129–133

F

family life, during WWII, 2–6
Fanning, Bill, 61–62, 66–67
Father Brown detective stories, 11
father of author
    illness of, 24
    during WWII, 3, 4
Fireworks: A History and Celebration
    (Plimpton), 118
fireworks industry, 118–119
FitzGerald, Patricia, 7
Flair (TV show), 68
Floyd, David, 42
FN rifle, Belgian, acquisition by
    NATO of, 37–38
Foer, Esther, 110, 118, 119
Fogarty, John, 106*ph*, 120
Ford, Gerald R., 113
Ford Foundation projects, 89
Fortune (magazine), 91–92
Frankfurter, Felix, 72, 92
Free Europe Press (FEP), 51–53
Fresh Kills landfill, redevelopment
    of, 178
Freyung, (West Germany), 51–53
From King to Congress (documentary
    film), 114–116
Fujian Province China, 127
Fuzhou (China), 128

G

Gamsakhurdia, Zviad, 121
Gates, Bill, 159
Gdansk (Poland)